PENGUIN CLASSICS

THREE SATIRES FROM ANCIENT KASHMIR

KSHEMENDRA lived in Kashmir circa 990–1070 CE. His literary output over at least three decades includes still-studied works on poetics and prosody, apart from devotional and didactic verse, mordant social satire and a lost history of the kings of Kashmir. Eighteen of these works were recovered in the past century, and another sixteen are known through citations. They have established Kshemendra as an important name in classical Sanskrit literature and a prolific and multifaceted writer on a wide variety of subjects.

A.N.D. HAKSAR is a well-known translator of Sanskrit classics. Educated at the universities of Allahabad and Oxford, he was for many years a career diplomat, serving as the Indian high commissioner to Kenya and the Seychelles, minister to the United States and ambassador to Portugal and Yugoslavia. Haksar's translations from the Sanskrit include *The Shattered Thigh and Other Plays, Tales of the Ten Princes, Hitopadesa, Simhasana Dvatrimsika, Subhashitavali* and *Kama Sutra*, all published as Penguin Classics.

Three Satires
From Ancient Kashmir

Kshemendra

Translated from the Sanskrit
with an introduction
by
A.N.D. Haksar

PENGUIN BOOKS

An imprint of Penguin Random House

PENGUIN BOOKS

USA | Canada | UK | Ireland | Australia
New Zealand | India | South Africa | China | Singapore

Penguin Books is part of the Penguin Random House group of companies
whose addresses can be found at global.penguinrandomhouse.com

Published by Penguin Random House India Pvt. Ltd
4th Floor, Capital Tower 1, MG Road,
Gurugram 122 002, Haryana, India

First published by Penguin Books India 2011

10 9 8 7 6 5 4 3 2

ISBN 9780143063230

Typeset in Sabon by Inosoft Systems, Noida
Printed at Manipal Technologies Limited, India

www.penguin.co.in

This is a legitimate digitally printed version of the book and therefore might not
have certain extra finishing on the cover.

P.M.S.

With a villain, influential,
mad for money, base and cruel,
holding high office, O people,
alas, where will you go?
Deśopadeśa 1.17

CONTENTS

KALĀVILĀSA: A Dalliance with Deceptions

INTRODUCTION

Satire is seldom associated with Sanskrit in the current popular perception of the ancient language as one mainly of religion and philosophy. Prominent among its satirists is Kshemendra, the celebrated writer from Kashmir. Little translated, his work is virtually unknown today outside the world of specialists. These were among the reasons for the translations presented here. Others are the brilliance and modern readability of Kshemendra's satires, their contemporary resonance, and the pictures they provide of common life in Kashmir a thousand years ago.

The Satire in Sanskrit

Though relatively few examples are cited in some scholarly accounts, the tradition of satire in classical Sanskrit is old and distinct. The earliest known of such works date to around the first century CE. They are *Ubhayābhisārikā* by Vararuchi and *Dhūrtaviṭasamvāda* by Ishvaradatta, a loose rendition of whose respective titles would be Both Girls Stepping Out and The Dialogue of a Conman and a Libertine. A third is *Padmaprābhritaka* or The Lotus Gift, attributed to Shudraka, author of the celebrated third-century play *Mricchakaṭika* or The Toy Cart.

All three are of the type *bhāṇa* or causerie. The setting of the first two is Pataliputra, then the royal capital near modern Patna. The third is set in Ujjayini, another important city. All satirize the urban lifestyle. Their characters include the parasitic libertine, the courtesan and her mother, a nun and a eunuch, a merchant and an actress, a rich banker's son, a swindler couple, an actor and a drama student, a tutor and a grammarian, and a poet and a chief of thieves. The descriptions spell out the foibles and the follies of metropolitan life as well as the social skills needed to deal with them.

The tradition continues with Shyamilaka's *Pādatāḍitaka* or The Kick, of about the fifth century CE. The work covers a cross-section of people in another imperial city, also including princes, generals, court officials and a Greek courtesan, apart from more common folk. This form of writing remained popular in later centuries, according to present academic opinion, and there are many examples of it, such as the twelfth-century *Karpūracharita* by Vatsaraja and the anonymous *Viṭanidrā* or The Parasite's Sleep, of about the fourteenth century, from Mahodaya in Kerala.[1]

Kshemendra

Kshemendra is a major figure in Sanskrit satire. He lived in Kashmir in the eleventh century CE and, unlike many authors from ancient India, has left some personal details in his various works—a few of which are also dated. Collated and cross-checked with other sources, such as

Kalhana's history of Kashmir, the *Rājataranginī*, written a century later, they provide an outline of his life and work.

The earliest date in Kshemendra's works corresponds to 1037 CE, and the last to 1066 CE, indicating virtually three decades of literary activity. Most of it took place during the reign of King Ananta (1028–63 CE) in Kashmir. Kshemendra names him as the ruler of the time in five of his works.[2] A sixth names his son and successor Kalasha (1063–87 CE).[3] It is surmised that the writer's birth and education took place before and during the time of Ananta's grandfather and predecessor King Sangramaraja. His own dates are estimated as roughly between 990 and 1070 CE.

Kshemendra was born into an old, cultured and affluent family supposedly descended from Narendra, a minister of the ninth-century king Jayapida. His grandfather was Sindhu, perhaps a high official of this name that Kalhana mentions. His father, Prakashendra, was a wealthy and pious man who devoted himself to religious rites and philanthropy. In describing these, Kshemendra gives a tender account of his death in ecstasy while at prayer.[4] His own son, Somendra, continued the family's scholarly tradition by adding material to one of his father's works.

Kshemendra's education was in keeping with this background. He mentions studying literature with the foremost teacher of his time, the celebrated Shaiva philosopher and literary exponent Abhinavagupta, who was active in Kashmir till about 1015.[5] Two other teachers he names are the poet Gangaka and the preceptor Soma. The second appears to have initiated him into Vaishnava studies.[6] A third was Manjubhadra or Viryabhadra, a distinguished scholar from Nepal, with whom he studied Buddhism.[7] His erudition was thus both varied and vast. He eulogizes two ancient poets: the sages Valmiki and Vyasa, the traditional composers of the *Rāmāyaṇa* and the *Mahābhārata*. His early work includes verse abridgements of both epics. Devoted in particular to the author of the second, he often uses the epithet Vyasadasa, the servant of Vyasa, for himself.

Apart from the rulers of the time, Kshemendra names some contemporaries associated with his writing. The two abstracts of the epics were prepared at the insistence of his friend, the brahmin Ramayasha, and his first dated work, an abridgement of Gunadhya's now lost *Brihatkathā*, at that of the scholar Devadhara. The Buddhist monk Nakka encouraged his later retelling of the *Jātaka* tales. A well-known work on poetics[8] was composed for Udayasimha, the son of his friend Ratnasimha, the ruler of Vijayapura. This prince, himself a poet, is mentioned by Kshemendra as his student and quoted in another of his works.[9] A second student he quotes there is the prince Lakshmanaditya.

Despite his princely friends and students, Kshemendra does not seem to have sought or received royal patronage as was the case with many men of letters in that age. While he refers, with due courtesies, to reigning monarchs in some of his works, in others there are neither such references, nor any eulogies indicative of patronage. The overall impression the works convey is that of an erudite and observant person of independent opinions and means, who engaged in literary and intellectual pursuits for their own sake.

Kshemendra's Work

Kshemendra's work was earlier known only from quotations in some anthologies and a reference in the *Rājataranginī*. In modern times, its first manuscript was discovered by A.C. Burnell, at Tanjore, in 1871. This was the *Brihatkathāmanjarī*, the abridgement of the lost work already mentioned. In the succeeding half-century, Indologists G. Bühler, A. Stein, B. Peterson, S.C. Das and M.S. Kaul located manuscripts of his other works, at different times, mainly in Kashmir. So far, eighteen of these have been found, and their texts edited and printed. Another sixteen are known, at least by title, from references or quotations in the discovered texts, but still remain lost. A list of all these works is given after the notes.

Of the now available works, three are the already mentioned abstracts, of the *Rāmāyana*, the *Mahābhārata* and the *Brihatkathā* respectively. Academic opinion considers them the product of Kshemendra's early years. The last mentioned bears a date corresponding to 1037 CE. Three other works deal with poetics and prosody. Still regarded as important contributions to these fields, they also provide valuable information about other writers in Sanskrit. Four are satires on contemporary life. Three of these are offered here; one I have translated earlier.[10] Of the remaining eight, five are didactic works on conduct and policy, and one a manual of rituals.[11] Finally, there are two devotional works: Kshemendra's long poetic narration of the Buddha's former lives and good deeds, dated to a year corresponding to 1052 CE, and his verse account of the ten incarnations of the god Vishnu, dated to 1066 CE, and regarded as the last of his known compositions.[12]

The sixteen works known only through reference and quotation include some plays and long poems, a satirical novel, a possible retelling in verse of Bana's *Kādambari*, and, what seems from the title, a commentary on the *Kāma Sūtra* of Vatsyayana. Also in this list is Kshemendra's history of Kashmir, the *Nripāvali*, which Kalhana described as the composition of a poet, but decried as full of errors.[13] While some of these works can perhaps be described with interesting details culled from the material available, further search for their manuscripts will hopefully continue.[14]

The existing Kshemendra corpus reflects a prolific and multifaceted writer. In the tradition of earlier Kashmiri savants like Anandavardhana and Abhinavagupta, he was both a notable poet and a seminal theorist of poetry. Though modern scholarship has generally lauded his contributions as manifold and important, it has tended to stress the historical and literary significance of his works on poetics. A wider view has also been expressed. For K.M. Panikkar, 'Kshemendra was perhaps the most comprehensive mind of his time, who wandered in every field, including satire, with distinction.'[15] For A.K. Warder, he 'stands in the first rank of satirists' and 'invites us to enjoy the multiple contrasts between the idealized or rather morally balanced world of legends and the bitter reality of contemporary society . . . for these we must recognize him among the greatest *kavis*.'[16]

The Present Satires

The satires presented here in translation are *Narma Mālā*, or A Garland of Mirth, in a free rendition of the title; *Kalāvilāsa*, or A Dalliance with Deceptions; and *Deśopadeśa*, or Advice from the Countryside. All three are composed in Sanskrit verse. The first consists of 406 stanzas, the second of 551 and the third of 304. The translation of all three is based on the original texts edited and published by Osmania University, Hyderabad, in 1961.[17] Most of the text has been rendered in prose for greater clarity and narrative continuity and cohesion. The concluding stanzas in all cases, and a few others of a descriptive or gnomic nature, have been translated in verse to convey some flavour of the original.

The three satires have stylistic similarities but differ in form and content. *Narma Mālā* could be a modern novella: it has a well-developed storyline that progresses smoothly from a beginning to a middle and an end in its three chapters. *Kalāvilāsa* has the traditional structure of stories flowing from a base story, generally two in the longer and one in the shorter of its nine illustrative chapters, with the tenth devoted to a didactic survey. *Deśopadeśa* has no overt narrative but consists mainly of aphoristic pen pictures in which, to quote a contemporary scholar, 'the characters and scenes presented are so vivid that they tend to turn into stories'.[18]

The style in all these works is marked by directness and economy. The narrative is terse, and the imagery brief and pointed, sometimes brutally so. The action is generally fast paced, except in passages of didactic elaboration. There are few scenic or allegoric descriptions in the conventional manner, and the verbal ornamentation in the *kāvya* style of the period is largely absent. An exception is Kshemendra's propensity for using puns to give double and satirically contrasting meanings to his words and even verses. A suitable translation of such *ślesha* into another language is always difficult. In some cases it has been explained with additional language or in the endnotes.

Another stylistic feature is Kshemendra's usage of unusual words and compounds, some untraceable in standard dictionaries, and others whose meaning occasionally needs inference. According to a recent study he 'does not refrain from words or idioms of his Kashmiri homeland, nor does he shrink from spicing his language with vulgar expressions'.[19] Though the first part of this comment needs more linguistic investigation, some of the vocabulary Kshemendra uses, while providing a contrast to the conventional classical idiom, does pose challenges to decorous translation.

These satires are set in the contemporary society of Kashmir. Some characters recur: the hypocritical priestly guru, the corrupt government official, the miserly and greedy merchant or banker, the courtesan with her retinue, the lascivious widow or housewife, and sharp professional practitioners such as the doctor or the astrologer. One character needing some explanation is the *viṭa*, here translated as the parasitic libertine. He is a pleasure-loving man about town, often impoverished and reduced to acting as a courtesan's agent. Some others, who feature only in one satire, include interesting types like the monastic scholar, the foreign student and the rich old man with a young wife.

Unlike some of Kshemendra's other compositions, none of these three satires bears a date. According to one scholarly opinion, *Kalāvilāsa* 'is perhaps one of Kshemendra's earliest works,' though 'on vague stylistic grounds it is usually supposed that *Deśopadeśa* is earlier'.[20] Any chronological judgement would, of course, be speculative in the absence of data. *Kalāvilāsa* gives the overall impression of a style more nuanced and courtly than that of the other two works, where it is sharper, more irate and acerbic. Whether this reflects, in any way, a progressive hardening of Kshemendra's views, or a change the other way round, can only be guesswork with our present information.

Kshemendra's Times

The century prior to Kshemendra's was a time of alternating periods of political stability and turbulence in Kashmir. Kalhana's history, written just two hundred years later, carries a detailed account of both. The accession of a new dynasty under Sangramaraja began with another transitional phase, when his army, sent to assist the neighbouring Shahi kingdom, in modern Afghanistan, against Sultan Mahmud of Ghazni, was defeated by the invader. Mahmud later also advanced on Kashmir, but then turned back. Meanwhile, the new monarch consolidated his rule, a process that continued under his grandson, the king who was Kshemendra's contemporary.

Despite internal power struggles, aggravated by an influential landed gentry and groups of mercenary forces, Kshemendra's time seems to have been one of relative tranquillity and prosperity in Kashmir. He refers to the kingdom as 'in the forefront of prosperous lands, adorned by savants and sages'.[21] Its rich life is evident from Kalhana's account, supplemented by other literary and archaeological evidence. Trade and agriculture flourished; temples and monasteries were built; there was contact with other lands and people. Travel to and from other regions may have shrunk compared with earlier times, but was still considerable—especially to trade in salt, of which there was no local production, and for higher studies, which attracted foreign students.

It was also a time of substantial literary activity in Kashmir. Somadeva, a younger contemporary, followed Kshemendra's abstract of the *Brihatkathā* with his own retelling some thirty years later. Prepared for his patron, Kalasha's mother, Queen Suryamati, this was the celebrated *Kathāsaritsāgara*. It is generally considered much better reading than the earlier abridgement, though it may be less faithful to the now lost original.

Among Kshemendra's other junior contemporaries was the writer Bilhana, author of *Vikramānkadevacharita*, the biography of a southern king in Karnataka, and the romantic poem *Chaurapanchāśikā*. Another was the rhetorician Mammata, who wrote the famous, and still-studied, work on poetics *Kāvyaprakaśa*. Two others were Kshemaraja and Bhaskara, both students of our satirist's old teacher Abhinavagupta, and respected commentators on Shaiva philosophy in separate works. That Sanskrit literature continued to flourish a century later is evident from the poet Mankha's account of a literary soirée, one also attended by Kalhana. From these and other such details it would appear that Kashmir was far from being a cultural backwater then—as it would be in later times—but was rather 'in the vanguard of Indian culture with notable contributions to every aspect of its life'.[22] Written in this ebullient age, Kshemendra's satires are also remarkable in their focus, not only on the ruling elite, but on the lives of more common people in society at large.

Narma Mālā

This is a satire on the bureaucracy of the time. It introduces the class with a wicked legend about its origin, and then narrows the focus to an existing hierarchy of its members and their activities. Finally, it narrates the rise and fall of a village officer in a setting enlivened by pungent portrayals of his superiors and subordinates, his wife, sister and children's tutor, and a religious rite conducted at his home by a guru with a motley retinue.

The story begins with the ironic assertion that King Ananta has relieved the distress of his people by removing the corrupt officials who are now no more than a memory. The author uses the word *kāyastha* to denote bureaucrats in general. According to academic opinion, the term in ancient Kashmir did not signify any particular caste, but was applied generally to officials in the king's service.[23] Kshemendra's caustic comments about their greed for money, inhuman extractive measures and dishonest habits are echoed in Kalhana's later history too. According to one study, such behaviour is also reflected in works of Sanskrit literature from other regions.[24] It is not very difficult for present-day readers to judge its resonance in our times.

Kalāvilāsa

The opening tale of this work has a rich merchant requesting an expert to instruct his son so that the young man does not fall prey to deception. The tales that follow elaborate on this theme, with accounts of hypocrisy and greed, lust and intoxication, and of the deeds of courtesans and bureaucrats, singers, goldsmiths and other swindlers. Most of the tales are further embellished with one or two sarcastic stories. The final chapter is a didactic survey of all the arts, good and bad.

The expert at the beginning of this satire is the legendary king of thieves, Muladeva, whose god is money.[25] This hero, also known from other literature, was the supposed author of a now lost work on burglary. Some of the tales that follow have also been traced to other sources: The story of Vasumati has one version in the Western *Brihatkathā*, and the story of Chyavana in the *Rigvedasamhitā* (VII.71.5).[26] The verse about the drops of ink from the bureaucrat's pen (Chapter 5.7) is telling enough to have found a place in later anthologies.[27] The enumeration of official trickery in the same chapter supplements the accounts in *Narma Mālā* as well. The topic of priestly humbug is also echoed in that work, as it is in *Deśopadeśa*, along with those of the cunning courtesan and the greedy miser.

Deśopadeśa

This work has been described as 'the broadest in scope of these satires [which] provides an introduction to the others'.[28] It consists of seven chapters, with separate portrayals of the villain, the miser, the courtesan, the bawd, the parasitic libertine, the student and the old man with a young wife. The eighth and final chapter has snide snapshots of the guru and an assortment of people who come to him. Many would seem etched from real life. Of particular interest are the student from a foreign land, the down-at-heel libertine and the *nirguta*, a low-grade former official, here loosely rendered as the pensioner. The tone of this satire is markedly bitter. The two verses that follow its epilogue, presented in the translation as a postscript, may possibly have a bearing on this. The historical background, known from Kalhana, is that King Ananta abdicated power to his son Kalasha and there was then a period of mutual conflict between the two, culminating in the former's suicide. According to a modern commentator, 'it is difficult to resist the idea that King Kalasha is blind with arrogance in the city and the abdicated Ananta is the bull in the village' in these stanzas. Also, that our author may be among the admirers bold in speech, though the same scholar acknowledges that 'all this is speculation'.[29]

Translation and Acknowledgements

Scholarly translations of the three texts, each by a different academic, have taken place at various institutions in recent decades.[30] The present work is intended to bring these ancient but still vivid and perceptive satires before the public readership of today. It endeavours to combine fidelity to the original with the requirements of modern English usage. The bulk of it is in prose for reasons already explained, but stanza numbers from the original verse text have been indicated within brackets at the end of each paragraph, to facilitate reference where needed.

The subheadings within the chapters of *Narma Mālā* are renditions of those that appear in the original text, except the first two in Chapter One and last four in Chapter Three, which I have devised and added to facilitate reading. In *Kalāvilāsa*, the first subheading in each chapter is a rendition of that chapter's title in the original; the rest I have devised. In *Deśopadeśa*, all subheadings are in accordance with the original, but I have introduced the last two to indicate the epilogue and the postscript. There is some inconclusive scholarly debate[31] over whether the subheadings in the Sanskrit texts of *Narma Mālā* and *Deśopadeśa* are later interpolations. Whatever its eventual outcome, they have been retained here for ease of reading. For the same reason the use of diacritics has been confined to the textual references in the Introduction and the Notes.

I have profited from the account of these satires in Dr A.K. Warder's monumental work *Indian Kāvya Literature*, the translation of the satires into Hindi with comments on contemporary society by Dr Moti Chandra[32] and the monograph on Kshemendra by Dr Braj Mohan Chaturvedi. Other useful works are the pioneering *Kshemendra Studies* by Dr Surya Kanta and the more recent study by Dr Uma Chakraborty. For a background of the period I have relied mainly on Dr S.C. Ray's *Early History and Culture of Kashmir* and Kalhana's *Rājataraṅgiṇi*, translated by R.S. Pandit.[33] Also invaluable was the glossary of difficult words used by Kshemendra, appended to the already mentioned Sanskrit text brought out by Osmania University.

I am grateful to R. Sivapriya, Managing Editor, Penguin Books India, for the initial discussion on this work and for giving me extended time to complete it. Thanks are due to Sushma Zutshi, Librarian, India International Centre, New Delhi, and her colleague Shafali Bhatt, for their help in enabling my access to the original texts and a variety of reference material, and to Sunil Kumar Sharma of the same library for preparing the photocopies. I acknowledge also the work of Ameya Nagarajan of Penguin Books India in copy-editing the typescript. The *Kalāvilāsa* translation was revised at the home of my daughter Sharada, and completed at that of my son Vikram and daughter-in-law Annika, to all of whom I send my love and thanks. Lastly, but most of all, I thank my dear wife Priti for her patient support, always helpful criticism of the drafts and unfailing encouragement, for which no words can ever be adequate.

Republic Day   A.N.D.H.
26 January 2011
New Delhi

NARMA MĀLĀ
A Garland of Mirth

Chapter One

Prologue

Victory to that lord supreme,
the illustrious bureaucrat,
infallible, who can at will
delude the whole world with deceptions. (1)

Kashmir is in the forefront of prosperous lands. Adorned by savants and sages, it even humbles the pride of paradise. Its king is the glorious Ananta,[1] whose mighty arms suppressed the machinations of ill-wishers, just as the god Trivikrama[2] did with the demon Bali. This discerning ruler also relieved the distress of his subjects by removing all wicked officials, who are now no more than a memory. A leading member of learned circles, one wise as well as playful, then urged a certain sincere and discriminating person to recount the past deeds of bureaucrats, both to deride their evil practices and for general amusement. (2–6)

The Advent

Salutations then to the architect of illusions, who created a world full of complexities and is responsible for their

3

origin, continuation and end. He has no beginning, but is everywhere. He has no attributes, but knows all the tricks. The controller of everything, he also swallows the deadliest poison.[3] (7–8)

When the all-powerful god Vishnu annihilated the demons in ancient times, the chief accountant of their households was so distressed that he renounced the world and took to asceticism. Ever hostile to the gods, he went to the banks of the Vaitarini, the river of hell in the nether world, and did penance there for a thousand years, subsisting all the while on mouthfuls of his own urine. Eventually he was able to propitiate Kali, the manifestation of the present Iron Age, which was then yet to dawn. (9–11)

Kali appeared before him, ready to bestow a boon. 'My child,' he told him, 'go to the earth and destroy all the gods. I give you this great weapon, the pen. With its strokes you will be able to deprive the celestial deities of the lamps and the incense, the floral offerings and the garments they are habituated to receive, and also ruin their temples. Covered with dust and surrounded by dogs, they will be reduced to wailing and crying even for their bread and water. With the disruption of priestly livelihood you thus cause, the sacrificial ceremonies performed in this world will cease and the gods will perish in heaven. Of this there is no doubt.' (12–14)

'As you wept in heaven when the demons were displaced, you will be known on earth as *divira*, which literally means "one who weeps in heaven" or "one who makes the heavens weep". This word also stands for an official. The black ink from your pen will engulf everything and also accomplish all your objectives. And in your line will be born many demons in the shape of officials who will come to acquire the wealth of this earth so that nothing of it remains elsewhere.' (15–17)

Kali then disappeared. As for the wicked-minded demon, he was reborn on earth after another age had passed. Sworn to overturn this world, he was born of a cruel butcher to the wife of a spade-wielding digger of pits. And he became the progenitor of a line which befriended no one. Vicious, sharp and rough, his progeny would ruin all livelihoods and loot everything, seizing everywhere properties both movable and immovable. Their limbs besmeared with ink, as if by a deathly embrace, they would be like the end of time. (18–21)

These were the bureaucrats. Soft when down and stern the moment they had the upper hand, they were many voiced while rendering service and many armed while hunting prey. Demonic, double faced and fault finding, they had a host of tricks for cheating others. The word for them, *kāyastha*, means literally 'in the body', but they are more like the ordure inside it. (22–23)

They soon infested the earth: cities and towns, villages and marketplaces. Kali now danced, dressed in birch-bark documents with scissors to trim them in hand, writing on the sky with an ink-filled pen, a briefcase under his arm. This great omnivore had come, sang fiendish Pishacha[4] hordes, to lay the world waste. And the officials, who plunder temples and deprive cows of their feed, began to eat and drink their fill, night and day. (24–26)

In bygone times, when the lord Vishnu bestrode the world, dharma itself had melted out of devotion and turned liquid.[5] Later, the world was overcome by the lord of bureaucrats, who are the disrupters of the daily and special rites of the gods, the divine serpents and all humankind. Then it was Kali who melted and became the ink which takes one to hell just as the river Ganga takes one to heaven. (27–29)

The Head of Domestic Affairs

Troubled by prominent villagers and afraid of being chained and beaten by them, the bureaucrat first took to other-worldliness and became a great exemplar of religious rites. Then he gave up rituals, went elsewhere and was, in due course, forgotten till he returned—an expert in documentation and indifferent to falsification. In time, appointed to office in villages, it was by a stroke of luck that he was put in charge of domestic affairs by the city's chief accountant, whom the hypocrite had impressed. (30–32)

Thereafter the earth was laid waste by his cruel minions, manifest bandits who acted on his orders. There were seven of them, all incarnate demons: Dambhadhvaja or Flag of Hypocrisy, Nishprapancha or No Explanation, Lubhaka or Hunter, Kalamakara or Wielder of the Pen, Suchimukha or Notebook Face, Bhurjagupta or Hidden Document, and Mahimanda or Scum of the Earth. 'There may be respectable people,' they would, boast, 'but they can all be plundered and destroyed.' They had eight Pishacha[6] fiends as their principal enforcers: Upatapa or Tormentor, Vajratapa or Thunderbolt, Parigha or Club, Dvarabhanjaka or Door Smasher, Dhumaketu or Smoking Tail, Kapimukha or Monkeyface, Kukshibheda or Womb Piercer, and Griholmukha or House Torcher. All eight went about, sticks in hand, to destroy this world of mortals. (33–37)

The bureaucrat himself is always surrounded by hundreds of attendants. He engages in hypocritical worship, reciting hymns with tear-filled eyes and many a sigh. His name is Mareecha and his praying is visible, well worded and attractive. But his thoughts are elsewhere. *'How many did I get killed in Vijayeshvara⁷ yesterday?'* he wonders, as he prays, 'victory to the Supreme Lord, delightful is his endless glory. *This move of three and seven will supersede things as they were in the beginning.* The Lord is filled with the riches of compassion, enlightenment and ultimate bliss. *The dead brahmins should be dragged out by their ankles with ropes from the place where they were killed.'* (38–41)

'Victory to the unconquerable Lord, whose greatness is illuminated by knowledge,' his prayer continues. *'Officials should go to such and such village to break the ovens there.* He is the likeness of all bliss, the source of all that is auspicious. *Those who oppose my punishment should have all their property confiscated and then be executed.* We bow to Brahman, the remover of all distress, who is manifest in consciousness. *People are like* guggulu⁸ *seeds: they yield their juices only when pressed hard.'* (42–44)

The bureaucrat Mareecha entered the assembly hall of his officials as it resounded with the singing of such hymns and the ringing of bells. It was the people's misfortune that, installed on the principal seat, he then saw his emissary, an officer who had come from a far-off place. This person wore a tall cap made of small felt pieces joined together, a soft tunic the colour of flax flowers and a thick cotton shawl scented with nutmeg and musk. On his finger was a triple ring of gold. Dirt still clung to his feet as he made a face and sighed to indicate his fatigue. He was the convener of a plan to plunder temples. Noting that this vile *bhagavata*[9] informer had arrived, the bureaucrat got up joyfully, and, taking him by the hand, seated him by his side. (45–50)

The Convener

We bow to informers, by whose grace officers have a thousand ears and eyes, even though they may be far away. The new arrival was meanwhile speaking to the bureaucrat. 'Having heard that you are now the focal point of all power,' he said, 'I am here to show you the way to the treasures of the temples. I will reveal all that there is in those houses of god: vestments, ornaments, jewellery and the rest. To your good fortune, the treasures in Vijayeshvara, Varaha, Martanda[10] and the other temples are such that they will satisfy even those who need no nurturing.' (51–54)

'A caretaker should immediately be appointed there,' he continued, 'one who is sharp, unafraid of slander and without scruples in sin. He should be a bureaucrat like yourself, sir: one who has earned repute without wealth, troublesome exertion or the plunder of property. He should be one who works merely out of devotion to his master, despoiling people, not caring if brahmins get murdered, to say nothing of cows. There may, of course, be others, but none to compare with him who would be

The Official Scribe

The official scribe, who had been sent for by the caretaker, then arrived. Dark and covered with dust, he was exceedingly thin. His stomach was sunken with hunger, his turban was full of holes, and his dirty tunic held together with a hundred patches. He wore an old and worn-out shawl, its end tucked under his arm, and the wretch had borrowed shoes that were painfully tight. Though extremely poor, he was proud of his writing skills. His steps faltered with joy at having been summoned after a long time. The caretaker's order was to him like a breath of fresh air is to a smothered snake. (71–74)

The scribe's wife had a tattered piece of cloth wrapped around her loins. The tip of her nose was smudged with soot. Her ears sported ornaments of clay. Half of a winnowing basket covered her head. She wheezed and often scratched her buttocks as her hungry child annoyed her. However, happy that her husband had obtained a position after so long, she now worshipped the god Ganapati with rice grains, incense and little cakes. (75–77)

Having noted down the messages with many meanings that his master had issued, the scribe was busy with fines. He wrote orders for them ceaselessly, his pen squeaking like a wounded monkey as it sped along. Counting the money with speed, he had soon given out two hundred orders. He wrote them for whatever the caretaker needed: stirring spoons, pillows, rugs, boxes, pots and pans. This made him a celebrity, and he soon became stout and

prepared to lead his own rich father into
death. And, if such a person were to follow
sir, then consider that, by the virtue of your m
home will become independently the reposit
treasures.' (55–59)

The great man took due note as all this was wh
repeatedly into his ear. 'Bring that man here qu
he told the convener, who went swiftly, returned
or thrice to show his respect, and then led in a wic
caretaker whom he had already prepared. (60–61)

The Caretaker

He wore a turban and a tunic of a jaundiced green colour.
His neck was stiff, as if held in a wooden splint, and his
unblinking gaze always turned upwards. A big fleshy
belly hung below. Arrogant and capable of great anger,
he seemed prepared to kill, like some terrible fever that
is troublesome, distressing and irremediable. (62–64)

In connivance with some intolerable libertine, he had
earlier gained control of many temples with ease. Now
he suddenly set off to collect dues, accompanied by
innumerable assistants, like trouble personified. 'He is the
cat-eyed demon Hiranyaksha,' people thought, 'who is
out to destroy the gods, having remembered his previous
enemity with them.' They fled from rich temples together
with the denizens of the shrines, while others joined the
caretaker's forces; his soldiers broke down the worn-out
doors and began a festival of plundering household effects
amidst the piteous weeping of frightened children and
housewives suddenly stripped naked. (65–70)

haughty, with his hands always full. He would look down as he reread the orders, or squint and knit his brows while making all kinds of faces. (78–82)

The Treasury Officer

The treasury officer then arrived. He had been invited by the temple priests and devotees to mediate the requisition arrangements. Proud of grinding down those on their last legs, this man had discarded his rags long ago. His turban spread across half his forehead like a leprous streak. The caretaker, who was bent on the elimination of the accumulated wealth of all temples, had already left many people with little more than ropes to commit suicide. The treasury officer now issued a long estimate of the revenue for the autumnal half-year. It included a collection of some four hundred and fifty thousand in cash. Once the estimate was accepted by the caretaker, who also seemed satisfied with his work and somewhat well disposed, the treasury officer asked about himself. (83–87)

'Many well-known caretakers of these temples opposed me,' he said, 'and they all left after selling off their own properties. But you, sir, I must help today out of affection; for our families share the same guru. Five or six good-for-nothing people accepted to the temple committee appropriate the entire money received, as donation for the gods and for the attendants' food. By the same token, you should take as your own whatever remains in the temples after the sales.' (88–91)

'Thus,' he continued, 'I took the great copper urn, and, with a hundredth part of it, devotedly had a bell made for the temple. In time, I sold the bell, and had a jar made with a part of the proceeds. That too was used up, gradually, and a small bell made with what remained. After some time, that was also broken, and a pair of miniature cymbals made, so that a little bit of the original bell is still preserved. A quadruple extraction can thus be made while offering worship to the god Shiva. I will also inform you about the grain stored in temples that you, sir, can buy and sell.' Told of many such methods, the caretaker soon emptied the temples, just as an old rat would a walnut. (92–96)

The Village Officer

An official was then appointed to look after the village. Avaricious by nature, he was clever at robbing good people. But this progeny of some shit-filled hell was like a water pot with a broken nozzle. He lived like a chicken inside its coop. The old, rattling door of his home was held together with string. His head wrapped in a piece of burnt blanket, his old and worn-out shoes chewed up by dogs, he walked slowly, with a limp, carrying a ragged shawl, a box with sesame seeds, sacred grass rings and clay, and a wooden vessel gnawed by rats. (97–101)

His conduct was correct. He would bathe, tell his beads as his beard quivered, and spend half the day reciting hymns at a temple. Bowing to the brahmins, circumambulating the cows, he observed the twelfth-day fast, ostentatiously giving a cowrie shell each to the poor people he saw on the way. (102–103)

It was by chance that the post of an officer had come his way. Soon, his house was filled with furniture and other goods. The neighbours, who would not give him even a burning coal in the winter, now offered him, unasked, all the clothes and ornaments he needed. His house acquired many servants. Its courtyard was whitewashed and the parlour painted with red lead. Sweetmeats gave new charm to his young wife, who began to look, within days, like a celestial nymph. (104–107)

Many things preceded him as he set out for the village: a sleeping mat of bamboo; a parasol, a pitcher and a copper bowl; a spear, a spittoon and a bell; a copper cup and a pair of shoes; a ladle, a pair of pourers, a case of birch-bark and a ritual footrest; a rosary and an ink pot; a mirror and a bathing vest; a casket and a cap; a sword and sandals; a book of incantations and an ephemeris; a sword blade and a red blanket; a sacred thread and a lute; a needle, and scissors for trimming the pen; a talking bird, an amulet made of lac, a knife, and a yoga sash; a book of hymns and clay from the river Ganga; wood apples and earth from a ploughshare. All these goods had been collected from here and there, without any thought of returning them. He followed them, dressed in a thick, loose cloak, riding a rented horse. Spurring it repeatedly, his hand raised high; he twisted his mouth as if to scare the people. (108–115)

He entered the village in well-washed white clothes, like an old stork come to devour the rural fish. Treasures fit for the god of wealth himself appeared before him on the pretext of his food and a hundred other requirements.

All hail our master, the officer! Immersed in thoughts of loot, adept at organizing documents, enjoyer of the riches of hell, living away from his own spouse, he does not contribute to growth, only to shortage. Always unwell, he is never sorry. (116–119)

With his arrival, the village became almost an image of hell. Hundreds were exhausted and depressed. Thousands sought refuge in trees. What can be said of all the men he declared to be at fault? As punishment, he had their cattle locked up—even put to death. 'Confiscate! Arrest! Imprison! Destroy the house!' these were his terrible never-changing commands. There were five or six porters he always used like animals. They tirelessly carried to his house whatever he ordered: coins, ghee and honey; pepper, ginger and salt; lentils and walnuts; lotus stems and grape wine; sheep and fowl; blankets, shoes pointed like peacocks, beds and shelves; household utensils of copper, brass and iron. (120–125)

Any conciliatory recommendations he received in private from his superiors he spat upon, crushed and threw away. He was also a hypocrite. Feeding always on meat and ghee when by himself, when a royal officer was there, he ate only two ounces of lentils, and that too without salt. (126–127)

The Village Clerk

Removing the original official who was unable to control thievery, the village officer appointed instead the man's son, who was most adept in that work. This person was an expert in ambiguous writing, deceptive or clear. He wrote with his left hand as his right thumb had been cut off. Expeditiously released from a twelve-year imprisonment, the villain went quietly to the officer's house and commenced the arrangement of documents. (128–130)

Holding a jar of liquor between his knees, he would take a swig from time to time. Limited at first, the amount increased gradually as he wrote, his pen screeching like the loud hum of a cricket, with blood taken from his little finger to emphasize faint letters. He made both the normal and the special rituals of the brahmins, the cows and the gods disappear. Instead, he would ceaselessly sing in his harsh voice the shrill compositions in praise of the god Shiva by the illustrious Rugna Natha, the guru of the leather workers. He did this while picking fleas from his blanket and crushing them with his nails, sighing repeatedly as he condemned the world around himself, or joyfully balancing new expenses. (131–135)

Drunk on the liquor, he would tremble as if possessed by a vampire and throw off his garland of mango stalks. The sound of the thick birch-bark used for writing being torn moved him like music. His testicles stuck out of a hole in his ragged garments. An overturned pot full of ink stained his body as he danced, inebriated and almost naked, breaking the pitcher that was his seat. He was then like a risen fiend, covered with dust, filthy, and delighted to harm other people. Slapping his armpits for a long time he used them as drums in his solitude. (136–140)

The Bureaucrat's Wife

The officer was a plunderer. He was like a wind, blowing day and night to fan fires in the forest that is the people. Soon his house was filled with wealth. His wife carried herself like a queen when he was away. Bejewelled and garlanded, she spent time chewing betel leaves, looking at herself in the mirror, and gazing out at the highway. 'This necklace is a burden,' she would say. 'I do not like these ear ornaments of gold. This damned gold girdle is too heavy, fit only for merchant women. I prefer only this single string.' Who would not marvel at her arrogant words? (141–145)

Hail the lady ink, who grants success in all endeavours. Hail the mighty pen, the foundation of prosperity. She who used to drink from a cracked and rejoined stone cup the unfiltered liquor that she had begged, now savoured wine scented with musk. Looking from below at that bureaucrat beauty in her mansion, the daughters of the neighbours thought that she was a lady from a patrician family. (146–148)

Chapter Two

The Libertines

Tormented by youth and stricken by vanity, the bureaucrat's wife did not even look down at the ground. She had the eyes of a fawn. Though restricted by her parents-in-law, she liked music and song, enjoyed young neighbours, and was given to jokes and laughter. Her limbs were scented with a pleasing perfume. She did not wear a bodice, and would show off the roundness of her bosom by half-removing the sash looped over her head. Yawning and turning back with a ripple at her waist, she would look at people with roving eyes and sidelong glances. (1–4)

Libertines thought that this woman with wanton looks could be had without much effort. They began to pass by her house in a casual manner, dressed in colourful clothes, and spending money on fragrant oil, betel leaves, incense and the like. Though they were eager to get at his wife, their designs were actually centred on the official's wealth. To that end they smiled, made eyes and put on hundreds of airs. Like snakes, unknown even to the knowledgable, they moved in circles, looking for an opening, ready to bite. Two or three of these well-known fornicators gathered in a deserted temple to consider ways of making an approach. (5–9)

'There is no doubt that she will be easy to have,' said one libertine. 'How can she tolerate a husband who is old and bald and with such a paunch? He is, moreover, a greedy, jealous villain, unable to make love and always travelling. He farts all the time and smells like a goat in heat. She has no child, though she is neither barren nor too old. Nor does she appear immersed in some grief or hurt due to a previous passion, a reason for which even women of loose character cannot be had.' (10–13)

'Your thinking is objective, sir,' said the other. 'But we have to find some way to get near her and become acquainted. One cannot get to know another man's wife without an occasion: a wedding or a sacrifice, a pilgrimage or a temple festival. Then, looking at her for a long time while brushing back one's hair; demonstrating one's liberality; talking about her under some pretext to display one's own pleasure, good luck and success; speaking to her softly and listening to her with respect: all this is possible. It is then also possible to kiss and embrace her child while looking at her, show her designs of clothes and ornaments she may like, and present her with garlands and betel leaves as the acquaintance grows. Finally, one can reach the stage of pressing her hand near a wall, kissing her when no one else is there, touching her private parts, and then sex. All these are expedients to ruin her virtue. Which of them have I not used to possess an official's wife, one unchaste and always ready to come?' (14–19)

Another Opinion

'All this we can do,' said the third libertine. 'But there is one obstacle. It is the contrariness of fate. Its machinations are like those of the sharp-eyed Chitragupta, the clerk of hell, who terrorizes all creatures and is the death of those without merit. The last are reduced to being beasts of burden, with loads, chains and official orders of all kinds.' (20–22)

'If death is not fate's name,' he continued, 'then who kills people? If it is not illness, then who destroys a limb with paralysis? "How many died today?" fate asks again and again. It lives off the dead like a dog or a skull-gatherer in the cemetery. Its hands are outstretched to steal the lives of even good men. As for the wicked like us, it gives them just a one-way ticket to hell. It could be a brewer of liquor who lusts for his own daughter-in-law, for fate knows everything about everyone while exposing their misdemeanours.' (23–26)

'But,' he added, 'I have a powerful friend who is dear to the king. He can protect all lives merely with a word. He has saved many people: arsonists, murderers of women, children, cows and brahmins, and servants who act as informers.' (27–28)

The Nun

'This Buddhist nun has free access to the house of the officer's wife,' the libertines then considered. 'She is an adept in thunder rituals, and the mother of all the spells for seduction. Ever ready to be a procuress, she is an established go-between for lovers. For women seeking men, she is a veritable goddess. Her tricks would overcome even chaste matrons like Arundhati.[11] A whore of long standing, who considers the sacred river Ganga no better than straw, she can soon arrange what we want.' Speaking thus to each other, the rogues then proceeded to the old nun's home. (29–32)

The Children's Tutor

One day, the officer's wife was seen in her mansion by a resident of the monastery. He was a man well fed on monastic food, which had also restored his youth. He wore a tattoo and a long holy mark of unburnt sandalwood paste. Proud of the soft crackle of his peacock pointed shoes, his sash tucked under his arm, he would avoid the touch of even brahmins, and scolded people angrily with words like 'You son of a slave!' (33–35)

This man marvelled on seeing the woman and was suddenly bitten by Kama. He then got himself a position at the officer's house, on a monthly wage as the children's tutor, teaching them how to write. Having thus gained access, the rogue began to work carefully, even though he did not know the entire script and could only write slowly the sacred letter *Aum*. (36–38)

This tutor counted money in his mind. The curious women of the household would collect around him. He flaunted his knowledge, though all he knew was the hymn of the eight incarnations. 'I am the teacher,' he would say, and act even more haughty. 'May the Lord's feet protect us,' he would recite. 'They look after the lowest, release us from afterlife and help us on the way.' Giving such verses to the children for their writing boards, he worked for a year without arousing any suspicion, accumulating the money from his monthly wage. Busy with spinning and sewing, drawing pictures and giving medicine, he had no time for the boys. If they called out, 'Tutor!' he would get angry and retort sternly, 'Am I your singer or cobbler?' (39–46)

The officer's wife saw the tutor. He would smile, talk with a grin, and try repeatedly to arrange a meeting. But she would not respond. He understood the language of women, and would still ask 'What does she say?' playfully raising his eyebrows. Finally, tired of the jests, the laughter and the ridiculous mockery of proud women, he would just laugh it away. (47–49)

'This gentleman knows and understands nothing,' the household women thought, and they dispensed with all shame in his presence, even to the extent of going about without their clothes. Meanwhile this experienced voluptuary behaved like the sage Rishyashringa[12] and fondled their breasts. Soon he began to act like a young stud stallion in a herd of mares, and began to service all the officer's womenfolk: his sisters-in-law, his sister, even his doe-eyed wife and others he had lusted after. Initiated by this lover guru, they all became unchaste and totally promiscuous. (50–54)

The Return

Meanwhile, the cunning libertines had also done their work, through the Buddhist nun and go-between, and begun to enjoy the officer's wanton wife, who had become quite independent. But the officer came back earlier than expected. Thinking of his young darling with great eagerness, he returned to the village on the pretext of some non-existent work, wearing a fine robe that he had hired. (55–56)

He had returned after a long time. His house was filled with ghee and honey brought for his service by the porters of frightened rich people. However, his wife glared at this fat rustic as if he were sick with dropsy. She now had many lovers. She laughed with one eye but wept with the other as she saw the wealth of sheep and ghee, cane, whey and honey at the house. 'I bought these beautiful clothes and ornaments for you,' the officer said, but she acted superior, as if she had heard nothing. Pretending a headache, she put on an oil-soaked bandage, and, groaning loudly, refused to come near her husband. (57–61)

Thereafter, there was a great festival in the officer's house, with all the village servants engrossed in making much noise. At its end, the officer, stuffed with huge quantities of rice and drunk on red wine, proceeded to bed like another Kumbhakarna.[13] But his wife, who had passed the day miserably, was repulsed by his embraces that night. She turned her face away from his kisses, prevented his touching her loins, crossed her thighs and lay motionless, pretending to sleep because she was fatigued from all that had happened in the house. (62–65)

The next morning, while his documents, vessels and other things were before her, she claimed to be unwell, complaining of a pain in her whole body. Her attendants then summoned a doctor. A person who loved his liquor and meat, he came straightaway, believing that fate had brought a treasure within his reach. (66–67)

The Doctor

Bow to the doctor. Devoid of knowledge and doer of dishonourable deeds, he strikes, like a serpent, many people with untimely death. (68)

He comes panting and repeatedly wiping the perspiration off his brow with his hand, as if overburdened with visiting a hundred houses at speed. He carries a paper marked with medicaments and their applications, and approved in advance by fatality. For he is a remover not of people's ailments, but of their money, and will never abandon them, just like the spear-wielding god of death who stays with one for life. (69–71)

As with infernal poison, snakes or vampires, the doctor may be propitiated with a quantity of flesh. He is the wrathful wind that withers age. A touch of his hand cleans the three humours, but destroys the organs. Why is he called a teacher of life? It is because he admonishes men to give up things. 'You did not stay or eat or drink as you should,' he tells them. He lives off the sick, and makes an effort to keep them so. When people are unwell from overeating at civic feasts, weddings and expeditions, it is a gift from the stars for the doctor. It is then he, not the fever, that eats much, disturbs the three humours, touches women's private parts and takes lives away. It is ignorant doctors, powerful bureaucrats and immoral gurus who are the cause of a people's decay. (72–77)

After coming in, the doctor felt the lady's firm, well-developed breast, which had earlier been fondled by others even more villainous. 'She cannot tolerate fasting,' he said. 'A tonic will not be good in her pain. Her mind is stupefied and her essential fluids affected. So I think she should eat with me. The best to begin with will be yoghurt thickened with sugar.' After this medical opinion, the attendant women quickly summoned an astrologer, who also came post-haste. (78–81)

The Astrologer

Bow to that eye of wisdom, the expert in the science of astrology. He has no learning, so goes about asking knowledgeable fishermen if it will rain or not. He has never even tried to calculate the configurations of the stars and the planets, but still carries some dirty papers to pretend to a knowledge of the past and the future. (82–83)

'You are likely to have some financial expense within the next three years,' he tells the enquirer. 'Also a fever, an ailment of the eye and an unexpected profit. Your enemies will not acknowledge any help you gave them, but it will not affect your person. You look weak, brother. Why not eat some broth? Indeed, it may even be jaundice, but that I will dispel with an incantation.' Thus does he trick dull wits, using ordinary knowledge of charms and medicaments mixed with astrological calculations. (84–86)

This rascal had already come to know, from hearsay, of the condition of the officer's wife. Even so, he made the pretence of drawing a chart of her horoscope on the dusty ground. As the officer placed an offering of coins and flowers upon it, the hypocrite sat motionless for a long while, counting his take on his fingers. Then, eyebrows raised, he said softly, 'This woman's face is pale. She is afflicted by a desire for sex. The evil spirit that creates this desire is very hard to exorcise. It possessed her when she was bathing naked in an empty room. This I see from the position of the planet Shukra, that is, Venus, in the horoscope.' (87–91)

The Straw-carrier's Message

The astrologer departed after proposing a ceremony for the worship of Shukra. Then a villager appeared, carrying a bundle of straw. His feet spattered with dust, he was covered in a worn-out blanket, with a rope tied around his waist. The man gave the officer a letter the officer's assistant had sent. (92–93)

'Ten cows were seized by the foot soldiers in lieu of the sheep,' the letter read. 'Of these, five are dead; and the remaining five have been confined to a barn. It will take three days to get them released if the helpers come soon. Even if they do not, you will still stand to gain, as a fine can then be levied from the village. As for that sharp brahmin, jailed on account of the pipe of ghee, he went on fast and has now died. I have arrested his wife, sealed the entire house and sent a list of his valuables to Your Honour. I have also stored in that house the comestibles for the porters that the caretaker had sanctioned for their monthly wages. So there is plenty of grain, and you should come here soon. This is my report to Your Honour, given on Sunday, the month of Jyeshtha.' (94–99)

The Guru

The officer read the letter joyfully and praised his assistant's efficiency. He had previously been a Buddhist, and then a make-believe worshipper of the god Vishnu. In order to safeguard his wife's health, he now turned, with all respect, to the scriptures of the Kaulas.[14] For this he invited a guru, a proud and greedy hypocrite who misled eager people with initiations and ordinations. (100–102)

We salute you, lord guru, agitator of emotions, robber of one's wealth and wife, all-devouring like the evil spirit which forages at night. His forehead bears a sacred mark, made of red paint, extending halfway to his lips. His skull and broad brow are moist with the droplets of water shed from a wreath of leaves and flowers. His head is bald, the hair growing only behind the ears and tied in a little bun. His earlobes are daubed with saffron. His eyes are glassy, and his chin, protruding. He lisps a bit when speaking at length, his mouth twitching like the cunt of an old she-buffalo. (103–106)

With what can the enormity of his mouth be compared?
He drinks a whole pot of wine within moments. The fetid
aroma of meat and liquor pollutes the meditation sash
that covers his whole chest. The deep orifice of his navel
is filled with vermilion powder, and his great belly with
a mixture of sweetmeats, cakes and fish. The indigestion
caused by wine and meat causes unbearable smells, which
he releases with the loud rumblings of an overfull cloud.
He is the very image of an ogre. (107–110)

The guru arrived. Though his lack of learning was
profound, and his mind clouded by the fumes of alcohol,
he was egoism personified. His appearance was weighty,
as was his speech.[15] So were his belly and private parts,
his jaws, beard and buttocks. Heavy too in his sloth
and ignorance, he was devoid of good qualities, but
an expert in cheating whores, lechers and officials. Of
much weight in everything, he was strangely always
meagre in the great teachings propounded by the god
Shiva. (111–112)

Can there be any pure person on earth who will not
offer obeisance to this treasure house of impurities, the
guru? Everyone fell at his feet while he nodded proudly,
his head bobbing like a pot during an earthquake. Then
His Holiness explained to the officer the rules for a
sacrificial ceremony to safeguard his wife and increase his
fortune. He quickly wrote, in saffron, a short list of the
material needed, and departed with his attendants, saying
happily, 'I will come back in the morning.' (113–116)

The Assembly Secretary

The officer had formally invited his father-in-law to the sacrificial ceremony, and that sinner also arrived. He was the secretary of the assembly and the court of law. Salutations to this respected city father, who is a lover of pleasure. In his hands rests the earth, with its mountains, forests and woods. He is polite and speaks sweetly at first, but can no more give up his crooked ways than an old goat its twisted horns; and, with a pen tucked behind his ear and a birch-bark document in his hand, this secretary of the assembly had seized the world. If the great boar could not rescue it from his grasp,[16] that divine incarnation's play with the demons was no more then a farce. (117–121)

The secretary wants money. Getting up, with a hangover, from the bed of a harlot in the morning, he waits to see some lucky face or sign. The night he has spent in fornication, but see how he cleans his visage with clay at each daybreak. He bathes and spends much time telling his beads, with sacred grass and sesame seeds in hand; but he is thinking of secret signs, covers and suitable accomplices. Spitting at a brahmin before him, he promptly goes back into his house, and then returns, concerned about a loss. Desirous of wealth and success, he bows to the dog shit on the road, mistaking it for cow dung, and again to the sweeper woman with her basket. (122–126)

Having had some roast meat with a drink, he then proceeds to the assembly court, surrounded by minions who have come to him since the early morning. Pressed under the birch bark, the smell of his inkpot signals the imminence of some hellish situation. For he is like a shark in the sea that is the court, doing good people to death with the fangs that are his pen and the venom that is ink. As for those who sup with him, their ancestors weep as they fall face downwards from their vehicles in paradise. The drops of ink from his pen are like black tears shed by a plundered earth.[17] (127–131)

The Court Clerk

Delighted at seeing the prosperous home of his son-in-law, the assembly secretary wondered if luck would not earn him some payoff there. With him could be seen his fearsome record keeper, looking over the house as immovable property about to be brought down. (132–133)

A salute to these clerks who can be the causes of catastrophe. They are always depriving people of their goods, movable and immovable. A good person coming to court out of fear, or attracted by an auction, is swallowed by these clerks, as the sacrificial offerings made in the water are by the fish. They are like dogs maddened by blood. Together with their officers, they leave a person who is caught up in their auctions without even his bones. (134–136)

Rama never slew the real ogres: they are in fact these clerks of the court who always feed on human flesh. Who can believe their words? They make the victors into the vanquished and losers into winners. They say whatever they please. With auctions and call bells in their hearts, they will end as vampires surrounded by the guards of hell. (137–139)

Without a bribe, the clerk is simply asleep. The base villain can see but is blind, can speak but is dumb, and can hear but is deaf. Taking bribes, finding faults, harming good people, inciting payoffs and protecting fraud: these are the signs of a clerk. (140–141)

The brother of a sweeper woman who also danced, the man became a dancer in turn. A snake charmer thereafter, he went on to guard grain. Next he was the caretaker of a village temple, and then a lowly servant in a bureaucratic committee dealing with war and peace. Travelling as a messenger to the Dranga land got him the rank of clerk. His sons and grandsons were all twice-born in the court assembly. What else could happen to such scavengers and carriers of big bellows? They now carry pots to collect the money from payoffs. (142–145)

Chapter Three

The Guru's Retinue

All the officer's kinsmen and their bedecked womenfolk came to his house for the sacrificial ceremony. His assistants and boon companions had meanwhile organized the material on the guru's list. This included chalk and quicksilver, a golden measuring scale and a box for jewels. There were also red lead and other powders; yarn of five colours and rice flour; a white parasol and white garments; an awning with strings, a knife and arrows; a mirror and a pair of shears. Then, a banner and a fan; flowers and peacock feathers; parched grain, white mustard and ghee; wood apples and areca nuts, nutmeg and walnuts, and barley and rice; two copper jars for water and a deer skin; sesame seeds and oil; firewood and sacred grass; incense, saffron and camphor; holy herbs and sandalwood; wooden sandals, a stool and a bed; a bell, a pot and a pitcher; liquor and meat; cakes and wine; onions, fish and cooked rice; tasty edible sweetmeats, crushed and roasted, juicy and fresh; bowls of piquant sauces, rice pudding, khichri and yoghurt. Finally, ten black goats and ten white, fourteen sheep and bellows for the fire. (1–8)

A disciple then prepared carefully on the ground, with powdered red lead, a *mandala* circle decorated with images of male and female genitalia. The guru himself came there slowly. An acolyte held his left arm, and another, the right. He did not look around; his eyes closed as if with some inner bliss. And, like some fierce chief set on plunder, he was followed by more than a hundred disciples. Among them were a tanner and a butcher; a potter and a fisherman; a marketplace hermit and an aged courtesan; a distiller, a liquor vendor and an aged gallant; five ailing libertines, three salesmen and a cook; a beef-eating Bhairava master, a Kaula preceptor and a weaver; a water-carrier with a mutilated nose, wearing *rudraksha* beads as a crest and ringing three bells; a Shaiva teacher greatly given to religious vows and also to the use of his mouth as a vagina. (9–15)

There was also a naked maker of occasional vows, one of which is silence; a composer of hymns with bells at his knees; two or three mad women surrounded by dogs; a crazy exorcist smeared with ordure; an alchemist, a magician dressed in vines, and an adept in the sciences of pleasure. And there were others, cunning servants of the guru, who attended to his food and drink. They all came in, maddened by the fragrances of the feast. Omnivorous devourers of food both cooked and raw, they made a clean sweep of the sesame, the ghee and the incense. One or two, and later many of them, also took away the rice flour, barley, wood apples, walnuts, ghee and the sandalwood paste, in bags and other containers. (16–20)

The Widow

The officer then had his own sister placed to service the guru's sacrificial rite. She was a widow who had observed the holy vows since childhood. (21)

All victory to the young widow! Her face is a lotus flower that outdoes the moon in its glow. Fiercely proud, she seems out of sorts without a strong rubbing-down. Her hips are large, her thighs and breasts plump, and her eyes like those of a doe. To see her is a tonic. With loosened hair flowing over her shoulders, she shimmers like a blooming lily surrounded by a swarm of bees. Her throat is unadorned but lovely, and her ears bare but beautiful. Down below it is as glorious as gold. She gave up wearing jewellery and uses no flowers or betel leaf—as if she was made, by the creator, out of sheer charm. For a shapely girl needs no necklace; one with nice hair, no flowers; and one with pretty eyes, no mascara. For what, then, would this widow need ornamentation? (22–28)

As mature libertines say, 'Without a widow there can be neither dharma, nor pleasure nor any salvation.' On seeing a youth she may outwardly wrinkle her brow, but her mind delights in thinking of an embrace. She dwells on the bliss of making love in her ample thighs and breasts, and caresses her secret parts at night with a sigh. And, as she casts sidelong glances at some good-looking young man, her sexual fluid flows like milk from a cow, while her pale, plump and shaven pubis gleams like the golden slope of Mount Meru grazed clean by the stallions of the sun. Thus, even if a man had an erection as large as that of a horse, it is questionable whether he could satisfy her while making love. (29–34)

Lucky are the simple brahmins and the long-haired ascetics into whose clutches some ardent widow falls during religious ceremonies. With a flower tucked in his hair and a tuft of sacred grass behind his ear, the young brahmin lover of a widow is comparable to the god of love. To this fierce celibate, with his heavy staff held high, the widow always provides the ritual food with devotion and faith. She follows him during journeys on pilgrimage, carrying sacrificial incense in a cup made of rhinoceros horn. And at night, the organs of both widow and celibate are mutually engaged, causing the earth to shake. (35–39)

Bow to the celibate brahmin, a storehouse of hypocrisy. The day he spends in pilgrimage, the night, in excited fornication with the widow. She, on her part, goes to the guru's house for her husband's death anniversary, but has her middle massaged in pitiless copulation. Engaged in sacred rituals for the deceased, she offers, without any hesitation, a feast of love to the ascetics at night. Locking her house on the pretext of praying to the phallic form of Shiva, she satisfies her own itches with a phallus made of leather. (40–44)

The guru and his disciples were beside themselves at the prospect of being served by this doe-eyed beauty. She was to them like cream to the famished, and they drank her in with their eyes. (45–46)

The Officer's Domestic Rite

The men awaiting initiation then came in. Their eyes were blindfolded, as if in the darkness of some vain delusion. An ascetic from the marketplace knelt down, clasped his hands, and addressed the officer's revered guru. 'Master,' he said, 'you have long been preoccupied with this ceremony. Other disciples are waiting, eager to participate in the festivity. This great man is well known for the religious rites held at his home. He is ready to start the sacrifice and now awaits Your Holiness. He has murdered brahmins and committed countless other sins. All have been obliterated with a single chime from the bell of Your Holiness. Therefore he regards all wickedness and destruction as no more than straw, as long as your serpentine hand rests upon his head. Having, by your grace, overcome the condition in which he was, he now steals everything, even from the temple of Shiva to whom he offers worship. Plunder of property, denuding brahmins, religious good works: whatever he does is but as you wish.' (47–53)

The Courtesan

'This courtesan has come to invite you, master,' the ascetic continued. 'You are kind to disciples, so please consecrate the water pitcher at her home. She has reduced rich lovers to mere bones, bewitching them with the powders Your Holiness has always given her. She cheats customers. Her tongue, lips and hands are worn out with the oaths she swears on cemeteries and treasuries. It is only your protection that keeps her safe. Her well-oiled face is smooth, but her eyes are hard. She has no reservations about outcastes, only about those who lack money. If time can be merciful, if a bureaucrat will not steal and if her king can have good feelings, then perhaps even a courtesan can fall in love.' (54–58)

The Oculist

'This doctor of the eyes has also arrived,' the ascetic added. 'A wretch friendly with everyone, he has blinded the whole world with his arrowheads and ointments. The abundance of eye ailments in the summer is like an autumn harvest for him. "Wrap up the sacrifice with a continuous offering of the white creeper," he says.' (59–60)

The Surgeon

'This surgeon,' the ascetic continued, 'also makes a living as a barber. His nasty ointments have made men's testicles grow to the size of plates. But he is a hard-headed man. If the price is high enough he will even use a piece of flesh from his own wife's genitals to rejoin a nose. While searching for rice gruel and other food, he had earlier installed an image of the goddess Chamunda, and would like you to conduct a sacrifice on that anniversary.' (61–63)

The Old Merchant

'And this is a very rich and aged merchant,' said the ascetic. 'He has a young wife, but lacks virility and seeks some aphrodisiac. But how can a young woman enjoy an old man? He drools, his eyes water, his breath rumbles and his penis hangs loose. Smearing it with balms recommended to him by old voluptuaries, this ancient always distresses his wife. Even if he gets it up with an effort, and mounts her to make love, he keeps thinking about his debts like an insolvent and gets no sleep. So, he presses it down, and puts his hand upon her crotch, guarding it like a treasure. Intending to have sex, he had eaten meat, milk and ghee, but vomited it at night. Or it was an attack of cholera? The girl is mortified to see her venerable husband looking like a dried-up skin in public.' (64–70)

'A daytime bandit in the dirty field of money, this merchant has swallowed up the deposits of numerous people. An anonymous purveyor of wood and straw described as actual goods, he is a crooked snake of this Kali age, and dances when the times are troubled. But his darling wants a young man, and the old husband stares at her like someone famished looking at a tasty dish from afar. Therefore, please call a flower-seller and make an incantation by which his potency will be restored and his spouse begin to love him.' (71–74)

The Ceremony

The guru listened to his ascetic pupil's representations and raised his eyebrows. 'I will do everything,' he said. Meanwhile, the disciples had already prepared a large sacrificial vessel for Shiva. It was the end of the day and, together with the guru, they then ate and drank for a long time. The wine they left was worshipped and thereafter consumed in large quantities by the officer's women and all his friends and kinsfolk. Some began to sing, and some, to weep loudly. Others wandered here and there and jumped about. Yet others imitated ecstatic devotion, and lay motionless, like corpses. Some were drunk, and, their garlands swinging, would embrace other men and even kiss the women. (75–80)

The guru himself was intoxicated. He sang a poem in the language of his country to the intense sounds of the lute, the flute and the drum. Getting up slowly from his seat, he then danced, blissfully raising one arm and the other hand, followed by both. His disciples also stood up, amidst peals of wild laughter. The garments at their waists began to slip as they made to hug the women. As midnight passed and the lamps went out gradually, their feast of love became a free-for-all. (81–84)

Then it was morning. The guru arose quickly and installed the ritual pot of water. He then got ready to go, as he was already invited by other devotees. Indeed, the earth is full of gold for gurus in springtime, as it is for doctors in times of illness and for officials at the autumn harvest. (85–86)

A Crisis

Meanwhile, one of the officer's men had arrived. He was gasping, trembling, almost about to burst as he looked around. 'Last night at midnight,' he cried, 'the Head of Domestic Affairs decamped with his followers, after taking a large sum of money from the royal treasury. Without anyone speaking about it, the news of his flight has somehow spread from house to house among the officials connected with him. The soldiers arrested your master the caretaker, his face split open with their slaps, his excrement voided in his clothes. Please consider what to do in this terrible state of danger, before you too are arrested and taken away with your whiskers plucked out.' (87–91)

The guru and his disciples departed swiftly, even as this friend was speaking. The officer sighed. 'Alas,' he said unhappily, 'the times have turned bad. How terrible is this age of Kali, when dharma sinks and good people are totally destroyed.' But, even as he tried to flee with his followers, he was surrounded by the soldiers. His urine spurted out with fear. It was pitiful. All his property was confiscated by the king and he was put in jail for a long time. Eventually, his sister, the harlot, secured his release, by paying a sum of money. (92–95)

Decline and Fall

He now had no wealth, only visions, as he muttered to himself. Bowing to all and sundry, he became an affable

flatterer. The officer who once stood erect like a penis
was now, with the loss of his power, no more than an
old sack for the testicles. (96–98)

Imprisonment is always the best salve to clear eyes
filled with wrath and blinded by the toxin of authority.
One who was contemptuous of the distressed, even of
respectable people who fell at his feet, will himself, when
out of office, bow before feet smeared with shit. An
officer's glory is, alas, as fleeting as a flame on burning
straw: there for an hour and gone the next. (99–100)

His wife went away. Penniless, but still greedy, he
wandered about the homes of his kinsfolk in search
of food. Unkempt, emaciated and extremely dirty, his
garments scorched and patched, he became, in just a
few days, as unpleasant a sight as a ghoul. His belly,
balls and heels were scorched with the burning husk
he carried in a little pot. A string was wound about his
knee to suppress the pain of gout. (101–103)

One, who used to seize the wealth of the gods and
the twice-born and loot village granaries, was now
famished—with a sunken stomach and a mouth gone dry.
While wandering about he fell into a latrine. Dogs bit his
feet and knees, and he bled a great deal. Kind people
gave him balls of leftover rice, on which he subsisted.
His head, shoulders, chest and sides smeared with ash,
he was past all shame; his hairy privates sticking out
of his half-burnt loincloth. He would wail for rice gruel
when someone gave him a piece of bread. The woman
who minds the water refused him a drink, thinking he
was an unclean outcaste. (104–107)

In winter he would cover himself with the straw
discarded by menstruating women, and fight for

earthenware plates and potsherds with beggar boys. The outcastes, who performed the rites for the dead, beat him with sticks. Blows from their braziers singed his eyebrows, beard and eyes. He lay in the mud, on the road, in hope of sacred rites. Finally, he fell on his face into a sewer of human excrement, his waist above him. There that base man's life forsook him. He went bodily to hell; only his bones were left behind. And thus did the fire of officers and clerks gradually go out. Freed of its flames, good people rejoiced and were content. (108–112)

Epilogue

This *Narma Mālā*, of Mirth a Garland,
discusses the misdemeanours
of officers, clerks and many others
who may act in wicked ways.
Composed for the recreation
of good people and to provide
them laughs, it also contains,
for all, some fruitful counsel. (113)

KALĀVILĀSA
A Dalliance with Deceptions

Chapter One

The Story of Humbug

Vishala[1] is a splendid city. The agreeable embrace of affluence has made it a home for all good fortune. It sparkles with jewels like the breast of Shripati, the divine lord of prosperity. Pearls hang in masses from its buildings, reflected in their gem-paved grounds as if on the multiple hoods of Shesha, the cosmic serpent. The glow of these crystalline mansions robs the night of its darkness. It is, alas, a real impediment for ladies out for trysts with lovers. (1–3)

For the city is an abode of Kama, the god of love. Though consumed like a moth in the flames of the great god Shiva's fiery gaze, he abides there in girls as radiant as the moon: in the nectar of their faces and in the breezes, ever-redolent of the fragrance of flowers from their loosened hair, that dry the beads of perspiration resulting from their exertions in love. (4–5)

In the lotus fields of the city there is the clamour of swans, eager for the plants' new shoots and petals. The sound reverberates like that of the anklets worn by Lakshmi, the goddess of prosperity. Young peacocks dance there like rows of turquoise fountains, presenting an image of the monsoon with its rainbows and multitudes of clouds. And in the crystal palaces flooded with moonlight gleam doe-eyed maidens, like celestial nymphs riding on the waves of an ocean of ambrosia. (6–8)

In that city lived the illustrious Muladeva,[2] the great authority on all the arts of deception. He had bested hundreds of rogues in trickery and earned enormous wealth on the basis of his own merits. Sought out by swindlers from all over, he lived in utmost magnificence, like a king. (9–10)

One day, when he was sitting with his friends after dinner, he was approached by the merchant Hiranya Gupta, who had come with his son Chandra Gupta. Received with due courtesy, the merchant saluted Muladeva, offered him a valuable gift of gems and gold, and addressed him after a moment's pause. (11–12)

'I am so conscious of your genius,' said the merchant, 'that in your presence my words can be no more eloquent than those of a village woman in a city. Your brilliant mind surpasses even the bright intellect of Brihaspati, the guru of the gods. It lights up people's hope as the sun does all the quarters.' (13–14)

'My treasury is full of all kinds of gems, pearls and gold, which I have earned with my labour,' he continued. 'This only son of mine was born in the evening of my life. Childhood is a time of folly. Passion maddens the mind in youth. Wealth is as fleeting as drops of water on lotus leaves quivering in the breeze. Doe-eyed women are its thieves. Scoundrels hover around it like bees on the lotus blooms of enjoyment. These traditional woes have also befallen my son.' (15–17)

'There is no way out for fools born in the home of a rich man. They become playthings in the hands of rogues, like gems in the ankle bells of harlots. Many are smooth talkers but, ignorant of the proper time and place, they become the prey of villains. Just like fledgling birds, unable to fly but still wanting to venture out for food, they are devoured by clever cats. This boy, learned sir, has come to you for refuge. Consider him your own child, and grant him full understanding so that he does not end up in some disaster.' (18–20)

The merchant had spoken with his head bent down in entreaty. Considering his words properly expressed, Muladeva broke his own silence with an affectionate reply. 'Your son may stay in my house as if it is his own,' he said. 'With an effort he will gradually learn all the secrets of trickery that I can teach him.' The wise merchant bowed in acknowledgement and, leaving his son at Muladeva's house as instructed, returned happily to his own. (21–23)

Meanwhile the light had faded. The sun, its glory dimmed, disappeared slowly from the sky like a gambler stripped bare by cheats. The maiden dusk came forth with the setting sun. She came with the elephant of darkness, but had a scarlet glow. Daylight, though forsaken by the sun every day, still follows him; not so scarlet dusk, for who can know a woman's heart? In any event, the evening colours also faded, and darkness spread gradually over the sky. The earth was covered by it, as if grieving at separation from the sun. One can even be in love with someone who is severe and always on the move. Then, suddenly, it was night. Ornamented by darkness like a forest maid with peacock feathers, it sparkled with the garlands of pearls, which are the stars. (24–29)

Moonlight spread gently. It awakens the night lilies, but also troubles birds looking for their mates and sets on fire the hearts of women whose husbands are travelling. The moon shone. It is the bright parasol of Kama, the pellucid mirror of the lady sky and the white beauty spot of the maiden night. It is like a royal swan sporting on the banks of the Milky Way. (30–32)

The night gloried in the moon as Kama does in the night. And the spring festival gloried in Kama. It is the time when the play of pleasantly intoxicated women becomes delightful. Swarms of gallants forsook the fading lotus flowers of the day and entered happily into the banks of blooming night lilies. The night was, in fact, adorned like a skull-bearing ascetic woman: ash-smeared with moonlight, wearing starry bone garlands and carrying the moon aloft like a charming cranium bowl. (33–35)

The full moon lit up the whole garden of Muladeva's mirrored mansion. There he sat in the moonlight, with his intimate friends, on a marble seat, surrounded by his disciples led by Kandali, answering their questions. With a long look at the merchant's son who sat in front, smiling so that his gleaming teeth outshone the moonlight, he said, 'Listen, son. This is the heart and essence of all trickery. It is extremely subtle. Once understood, even wealth based on unshakable foundations can be made subject to momentary whims.' (36–39)

'This world is a lonely wilderness,' Muladeva continued. 'It has wells hidden under a mesh of leaves and twigs, into which young and foolish deer can fall. The wells are strongholds of hypocrisy and humbug. By nature they lie deep within this world. Their mouths are like a pot of gold surrounded by coiled and cunning snakes. Humbug is a secret charm, a wish-granting jewel for much sought after treasures. It helps in acquiring wealth, even that of crooks and rogues.' (40–42)

'Who can know the ways of humbug?' he added. 'It is like a fish in the water, with no hands or feet; not even a head. It can even be invisible. Just as serpents are caught by charms, foolish deer, by snares, and birds, by nets, so are human beings trapped by humbug. All glory to it. Never perceived, it always dupes people. It is the beginning and the sustainer of illusion, and the first step in vanquishing the world. Illusion is hard to bear. It is like a serrated wheel with thousands of sharp teeth. Humbug is its axle and its base.' (43–46)

'Humbug is also like a tree. The eyes closed in prayer are its root, and the hair wet from a ritual bath, its water. Ceremonial purities are its flowers, and comforts the fruit on its many branches. Fasting and such observances are called the stork's humbug, and secret rules, that of the tortoise. Quiet movement with lowered eyes is the ultimate humbug, named after the cat.' (47–48)

'The stork's humbug is a lord of its kind, and that of the tortoise, a king. But the cat's is the emperor of all humbug. In this humbug the nails and beard are kept trimmed. The hair is done up in a crest, or it is twisted to hang between the brows. The body is smeared with clay, like a ghoul. The man takes trouble with his shoes and speaks very little. On his fingers he wears a ring of sacred grass with a fat knot, and round his neck a chain of gold. His arms are draped with the sash on his shoulder, as if he is carrying something valuable in his hands. He gesticulates with his fingers to assert his expertise in various disputations, and his lips move in some silent incantation, as he looks out at crowded city streets.' (49–52)

'Touching his earlobes repeatedly, he takes dramatic sips of sacred water and stays long immersed in some holy ford, holding up everyone else. His teeth chatter to show how hard it is to do this in the winter. There are extensive marks of religious ceremonies on his limbs, indicating that he has followed all the rituals in praying to the gods. He sticks a flower in his hair and casts his gaze all around him like a crow. Such is the appearance from which this hypocrite may be known.' (53–55)

'This humbug is a scoundrel in search of prestige and recognition. Indifferent to merit, he will fawn on those without it. Hostile to his own kin, he will exude fraternal compassion for outsiders. He is also pitiless. With bowed head, he will be all sweetness when it suits him. But once his purpose is served, he will only wrinkle his brow and say nothing.' (56–57)

'There was, in ancient times, a demon named Jambha, who usurped the riches of the gods,' Muladeva continued. 'He now lives on earth as deceit personified in humans. The humbugs of ritual purity and asceticism, and of priesthood and meditation, are not even a fraction of pure, effortless hypocrisy. That of purity will argue about permissible and polluting conduct, question even the ground one stands on, and physically touch only one's own kin. In this way it wants to replicate the sage Vishvamitra.' (58–60)

'Then there is the humbug of non-violence. He collects all kinds of goods, still wants more and looks out for pleasure. He exhibits himself everywhere, with shaven head or matted hair, naked or in ochre robes, carrying a staff or a sunshade. He may be emaciated like an ascetic, or fat and bald, with a scarf or even a high

turban covering his head. Greed is the father of humbug.
Delusion is the mother, fraud, the sibling and audacity,
the offspring.' (61–64)

The Birth of Humbug

In times bygone, the god of creation made the worlds
and all the creatures. His work completed, he rested for
a long time, absorbed in thought. With his divine sight
he saw people living helpless in the world, unable to
acquire wealth and enjoy pleasures just because they
were straightforward and honest. For a moment he closed
his eyes in search of a solution, full of illusion, to this
situation. Then he created humbug as a basis for the
prosperity of men. (65–67)

Humbug rose before him in priestly garb. He carried
sacred *kusha*[3] grass and a book, wore a garland and a
black deerskin, and was equipped with an empty vessel,
a small shovel, a staff and a horn as crooked as his own
heart. A thick piece of the sacred grass adorned his ear,
and another, twisted into a ring, his finger. He wore
on his shaven head a wreath of the same grass, with a
white flower stuck at its base. He was stiff-necked, and
his visage was wooden. His lips moved in some silent
recitation, and his eyes were closed, as if in meditation.
Beads of the *rudraksha* seed encircled his wrist, and his
hand bore a bowl filled with clay. A raised brow, a grunt
and an angry look from the corner of one eye conveyed
the impression of a wish to say something unpleasant.
But he kept silent, concerned for his ritual purity and

guarding himself from the touch of others even in that heaven of Brahma.[4] It seemed that he was anxious to be seated suitably. (68–72)

His remarkable appearance was so impressive that even the seven holy sages stood up to bow to him with clasped hands. The sage Agastya was struck by wonder at the extreme austerity of his deportment. The sage Vasishtha shrank with embarrassment at his own much lighter asceticism. Kautsa bewailed the simplicity of his personal penance and then shut up. Narada displayed contempt for his own practices devoid of any pomp. Jamadagni sank his head to his knees. Vishvamitra was terrified. Galava turned his face away. Bhrigu sank into himself. Even the god Brahma, who creates all things in a trice, silently stood up on seeing Humbug, so moved was he by respect, wonderment and joy. (73–77)

Humbug seemed upset at having to wait for long. He fixed his gaze on his progenitor and the god's lotus throne, and stood proud and motionless, as if impaled on a spear. The four-headed god realized that the newcomer wished to be seated. His teeth gleaming in a smile, as if at his carrier, the swan, he said kindly, 'Son, sit in my lap. You are worthy of it by virtue of the dignity that your great and remarkable austerity and other merits have given you.' (78–80)

On hearing these words, Humbug carefully sprinkled water on the creator god's lap to purify it, and quickly sat upon it. 'Do not speak loudly,' he said to the god, 'and if you have to, please cover your mouth with your hand so that your breath does not touch me.' Brahma smiled at this unparalleled concern for ritual purity. 'Humbug you certainly are!' he said with a wave of his hand. 'Arise.

Go to the sea-girdled earth and enjoy pleasures unknown even to the denizens of heaven.' (81–84)

Sent off thus with all respect, Humbug descended to the earth. He entered the ocean of worldly existence like a rock tied around the necks of mortals. Wandering in the world, its forests and cities, he arrived in the land of Gauda, and there unfurled his flag of victory. He then entered the speech of the Vahlikas, the fasting rituals of the eastern and the southern people, the privileges of the Kiras and everything of the Gaudas. (85–87)

All those who put on holy marks of consecrated ash after religious rites in the morning are Humbug's aides and assistants. He was quick to divide himself into thousands of entities in order to be among the people. He lives personified in the mouths of court officials and lawyers. He has found place in the hearts of teachers and children, ascetics and ordinands, and crooked government functionaries. He is also present in astrologers and doctors, merchants and goldsmiths, dancers and actors, preachers and singers, and servants and roadside performers. (88–91)

Having infected all mankind, hypocrisy also entered into birds and trees. The stork waits for long periods, motionless, on one foot, waiting for the fish at holy bathing places. Trees covered in roots and bark always endure the heat, the cold and the wind, wanting only water. Humbug is thus everywhere. This must be reflected upon, as a proper understanding of it can mitigate deception. For hypocrisy is the proverbial wish-fulfilling tree of all deceivers. Even the god Hari measured out the world in the deceptive garb of the dwarf incarnation, in ancient times. (92–96)

Chapter Two

Accounts of Greed

Greed must always
merit reflection.
Obsessed by it,
the greedy imperil
one everywhere.
For what should not
or should be done,
they just don't care.

The demon of acquisition and accumulation is the basic cause of greed. All-consuming, it works through deception, exchange, confusion, new distractions and fraud. Defeated by the virtuous, who observe the laws and are tranquil by disposition, greed burrowed into the pit that is a crooked tradesman's heart. (1–3)

Tradesmen rob people happily: with trickery during purchase and sale, with false measurements and custody of deposits. They steal in broad daylight. Stealing people's money by various fraudulent means, the tradesman is pained to part with no more than three coppers for the needs of his own household. He enjoys stories, and always goes to hear recitations from holy books. But he runs away from religious donation as if it were a black snake that might bite him. On sacred occasions like the twelfth of the fortnight, the father's day, the equinox or an eclipse, he takes a long ritual bath, but will not donate even a penny. Instead, casting furtive looks in all directions and hiding himself from seekers of alms, the crook flees, like a thief, through obscure lanes. (4–8)

The merchant is a villain. He will keep quiet while making a sale; will not speak even in reply. However, on seeing a person with something in hand to place on deposit, he will be eager to start a conversation. He will rise and bow, give that person a seat, ask about his welfare and then begin a pious dialogue. (9–10)

Someone comes to the merchant. 'Brother,' he says, 'I wanted to deposit this money and go away. But an unlucky conjunction of planets starts tomorrow morning. What should I do?' (11)

The merchant's eyes widen. He pretends to be sorry as he looks here and there, as if preoccupied. 'Good sir,' he replies eventually. 'This place is at your disposal. But it is hard to accept a deposit for long in these bad times. Even so, I am your servant.' (12–13)

'This *Bhadra* conjunction is not so bad,' he continues. 'It is auspicious for making deposits. This is the experience of many knowledgeable people. You know that too. A friend had once made a deposit on this very day. In time he took it back safely and without delay.' (14–15)

Plying that simple soul with such nonsense, the wicked fellow takes his pile of gold, his own mind overjoyed at the prospect of making a large profit from the purchase and sale of all kinds of goods with the money now obtained, and becoming an even richer merchant. (16–17)

But the jars filled with the unused wealth of miserly merchants waste away like the sad blossoming breasts of child widows. These merchants, always intent on hoarding wealth without using it for charity or pleasure, are like great rats in an old temple which is this world. In this world also roams an enormous serpent, evil and prickly, which is the local ruler. (18–20)

The depositor wandered all over, and, after a long time, chanced to return home. He was alone and had no money. 'Where has that good tradesman gone?' he hesitantly asked someone. 'Friend,' he was told, 'the wealth of that man is something else today. Trading in areca nuts, musk, sandalwood, camphor, pepper and all kinds of new cloth, he logs up millions in moments with just a stroke of his pen. He now lives in great comfort in that imposing mansion as high as a hill with lovely paintings hanging from its walls. Even the ruler of this place now seeks out this great man.' (21–24)

Shaking his head in wonder on hearing this, the man went to the merchant's house. There he stood for long at the gate, dejected, in his worn-out clothes. The merchant was behind the trellis that screened his large house. He gasped on recognizing the man, and was petrified, as if struck on the head by a thunderbolt. (25–26)

The man approached him haltingly, and, somehow finding an opportunity when they were alone, gave his name and asked for his deposit. Even as he spoke, the merchant raised his eyebrows, waved his hand and turned his face away. 'From where has he come, this wicked, lying, good-for-nothing?' he demanded. 'Who are you? From where have you appeared and at whose behest? I do not remember seeing you before, let alone speaking with you. O tell me when, where and who deposited what with whom?' (27–29)

'Just see, O people!' he ranted. 'What kind of times these are! How ill-omened and distressing! This man wants money from me, but you know everything. Deposits are never even accepted in our Haragupta family, to say nothing of the terrible sin of concealing them. Still, people given to complaining about their betters will always do so. As for you, give the date; see for yourself all that was written down on that day. My son writes the record of all transactions, as I am an old man.' (30–33)

Thus dismissed, the agitated man went to the son, who said, 'Father knows.' The father responded, 'My son knows.' Returning to the son, he was told, 'Father writes down everything': thus was he tossed from one to the other like a ball. Eventually, he went to the royal palace to get back what he had deposited before he went abroad. But the merchant will endure the king's anger without yielding even a part of the money. Though squeezed and threatened with various instruments of torture, he still insisted 'there is nothing that was deposited with me.' For they are greedy by nature, these people who thirst for the salt water called money. They will abandon their own bodies like so much straw, but not part with even a fraction of their cash. (34–37)

Shukra and Kubera

The god Kubera is the lord and repository of all wealth. Once, he was approached by his childhood friend, the sage Shukra, who wanted some money. (38)

'Comrade,' said Shukra, who was the guru of the demons, 'your great wealth surpasses that of both the gods and the demons. It is a source of joy for your friends and of grief for your enemies. I am your friend, lord of wealth, but, though burdened with a large family, I possess nothing. A friend who stands by one in one's joys and sorrows, of his own accord, is to be admired.' (39–40)

'Great men are born in noble families,' Shukra continued. 'Their fame commands respect. Their riches provide a living to many supplicants. Their comrades should be able to make use of their affluence. For friends and treasure, acquired through merit and preserved with great effort, protect one in both good times and bad.' (41–42)

The lord of wealth was torn between affection and greed. The guru of the demons had approached him lovingly and in private. He thought for a long time and replied, 'I know you as a childhood friend who loves me greatly. But I am unable to part with even the least bit of money as long as I live. People become friends for many reasons. Close ones seek affection. Wives and children are easy to have in this world. The only thing hard to get is money. To give it away requires great daring, and it is surprisingly difficult to do. One could well give up even the body but not the least bit of wealth.' (43–46)

Rejected by his friend, Shukra went away. His hopes had been dashed. His mind was awhirl and his face livid with shame. But he was a great yogi. After pondering over the matter for a long time with his aides at home, he used his magic powers and entered the god of wealth's heart to seize his unlimited riches. And Kubera, now possessed by Shukra, became extraordinarily generous. At the latter's signal he donated his entire wealth to the brahmins. (47–49)

Only after the demons' guru had left, after taking all his money away, did the god of wealth understand his magic. After thinking for a long time, he smote his brow, and, heaving hot sighs, spoke of Shukra's deception to his friends Shankha, Mukunda, Kunda, Padma and others. 'Friends,' he said, 'I have been cheated by the trickery of Shukra. He is a cunning magician who knows my weaknesses. He is also extremely greedy, and is hard to beat because of his demonic support.' (50–52)

'Now I have lost my wealth. Within moments I have become as worthless as a twig. With whom can I speak about this distress? What can I do, and where can I go? A person with no money is ostracized by the people. Without them, he suffers humiliations. And many are the problems of one humiliated. All those who love him and tend to him, as to a sacred vine, leave him when his wealth and life are gone. Wealth makes him learned and handsome, respectable and famous, noble and brave. Without it even his merits are counted as defects.' (53–56)

The anguish caused by the loss of wealth is hard to bear. His heart aflame with it, Kubera consulted his aides for a long while, and then sought refuge with the god Shiva. That great god is the sanctuary of the world. Told by this old friend of his situation, he sent an emissary to summon Shukra. (57–58)

Shukra came immediately on being summoned. He was gleaming with the glow of wealth as he stood before the great god, his hands raised in salute to his crown. 'Sir, you are a man of gratitude,' the god said to him. 'Yet you have cheated your friend, the god of wealth. Even ungrateful people do not go to this extent of being adversarial with friends. Only ingrates who do not care for their own reputations in changing their positions do this. He is an affectionate, well-wishing and loving friend. Your cheating him was not proper.' (59–61)

'You are a wise person,' the great god added. 'Was this deplorable act you committed in accordance with the scriptures, appropriate to your vows or in keeping with your lineage? Is it your prudence or self-restraint, the advice of your gurus or your own natural preference that has made you a cheat?' (62–63)

'To whom is money not dear?' said the god. 'Whose mind is not taken up by it? Yet those who seek the wealth of repute do not want ill-gotten gains. O do not tarnish the purity of your Bhrigu lineage with the dirt of greed. It will stain your standing, so far spotless like the royal swans. Besides this, what kind of a cheat among cheats is one who will forsake endless glory for wealth that is no more than a wisp of straw quivering in the wind? The crooked minds that discard good conduct to cheat others are actually foolish, for they cheat their own good deeds. Their reputations are ruined. Their prosperity, always delicate like a new shoot, is overcome by the odour of the poison tree that is scandal.' (64–68)

'Indeed, even the crystal-clear mirror of good men's glory is clouded by the sighs of people humiliated and distressed. Unclear minds sometimes do deeds out of carelessness; you can rectify this just by returning the money. You can cleanse, with your own hand, a once blameless reputation, now sullied by scandal. Do what I say, and give back Kubera's wealth.' (69–71)

Even though the god of gods and the father of the three worlds had said all this, so kindly, Shukra remained shackled by greed for the wealth of another. 'Lord,' he said with folded hands, 'your commands are honoured even by the gods. Who could ignore them without a care if he were not in a bad way? How can someone poor, with servants, women and children suffering at home, think of right and wrong in taking money? I always thought that my friend, the lord of wealth, would help me in my distress, and great were the hopes for this in my heart. So I went and begged him, discarding all shame. But he was even more shameless, and suddenly destroyed my hopes with his refusal.' (72–76)

'When a villain thus destroys hope with no care at all, he is fit to be struck without weapons, burnt without fire and killed without poison. He is then my enemy, and cheating such a one is not a sin but a good deed. Besides, a pauper's earning money, even by trickery, is not censurable. The truth Your Worship taught me was that wealth is not to be discarded, not even a particle of it. For, obtaining it is life, and life is harmed by abandoning it.' (77–79)

The god spoke several times to Shukra and made many requests. Then, angered by his continued refusal, he suddenly swallowed him. The fire inside his belly was terrible, like the conflagration at the end of time. Roasted in it, Shukra screamed and cried. Nevertheless, told repeatedly, even then, to return the money, he would only say, 'Lord, I may die, but I will not part with even a fraction of Kubera's wealth.' (80–82)

Shukra wept and cried excessively in the depths of Shiva's belly, engulfed in its fearful flames, which had flared even more with his arrival. 'Give up this obstinacy for another's money,' the god of gods told him, 'do not perish in the great fire within me.' But, though his bones were cracking and his tissues melting in the tremendous heat, Shukra merely sighed and said, 'I will die, but I will not give back even a particle of that wealth.' Eventually, when only moments remained of Shukra's life in that fire, he began to pray to the goddess Gauri, the spouse of Shiva. Pleased by her love and assured by her words, the god then let Shukra come out through the divine phallus, the passage way of something else with the same name.[5] (83–87)

Thus it is that the greedy by nature will endure the worst of torture but not part easily with money. Thus do crookedness, cunning and deceit, born of greed, live in avaricious hearts. But greed can never cheat those who refrain from succumbing to it. (88–89)

Chapter Three

Accounts of Lust

So seductive is lust that it totally confuses the mind. Like a sweet but insidious poison, it can even deprive one, suddenly, of life itself. Look at elephants in rut. The beasts are swiftly lured into traps by cow elephants. Then they suffer kicks, sharp pricks of the goad and fettering with chains. Scorched by desire and cheated by pleasure, what does the elephant not endure? (1–3)

Similarly, the man enslaved by pleasure, though long familiar with the wiles of women, is made by them to strut and dance like a pet peacock. To attract men can be an obsession with women. They steal the hearts of such fools with deception in the dark nights of male delusion. They are a vine of addiction; a snare for the antelope, passion; a chain to fetter the elephant which is the heart. Once in their power, who can hope to escape? (4–6)

Even the man who has conquered himself, who understands various worldly, divine and emotional illusions, cannot comprehend the deceptions of women. Their ways are extraordinary. With elegant behaviour and forms as delicate as flowers, whom can they not infatuate? But their hearts are as hard as a rock of adamant. They are indifferent to those who love them, and long for those who keep away. They are haughty with the meek, suspicious of good feelings and attracted to cheats. (7–9)

In this world, that man alone is master of his home who does not have a wife who is seen by everyone stretching her limbs voluptuously to attract others. As for the husbands overcome by passion, speechless and out of their senses, women throw the household sweepings in their faces. Even a matron puts on the airs of an innocent maid and asks such a foolish husband for the moon to wear as a beauty mark. And the husband, enslaved by her coquetry, massages her feet when this wanton is tired on return from a visit to her lover on the pretext of having gone on pilgrimage. (10–13)

It is in a woman's nature to be duplicitous. She looks at one man and speaks with another; with one she flirts and with another makes love. Base by temperament, she acts the elusive doe for her husband and the flitting bee for other blossoms. She is as false as a buzzing fly, and as crooked as a snake. Who can ever claim her as his own? (14–16).

'Blessed is the courtesan,' women sigh and say, 'she makes love freely with many young men, enjoying both pleasure and wealth.' A fickle-minded woman will stand inside her house, looking out at the street and singing unashamedly. She runs for no reason and laughs with her teeth gleaming like a string of crystal beads. 'This husband of mine knows nothing,' she tells her staff as she does the man's work, 'he acts just like an animal.' For, though alive, he may virtually be dead to her. She speaks loudly in the house, attends to those who come on business, and herself goes out to work. (17–19)

Jealous older wives, spouses of servants, or those of

officials, artisans and actors, are, by nature, dear to young men. So are the wives of greedy people and of travelling salesmen, and women who are party-goers. All these women tend to always run down their own husbands while praising the merits of others. (20–21)

The wife may be good-looking or not, but she has little money and many expenses. Her husband is a fool. She knows all the arts and likes to associate with base people. Given to gambling and drinking, she is skillful, enjoys songs and long stories, has many friends among whores, and is, by temperament, predisposed to military men. She neglects household work, dresses in many ways and has a flair for repartee. Shameless by nature, she is totally without restraint in her habits. (22–24)

Outwardly a saint, in private she likes all kinds of pleasurable activities. She asks, in loving and tender words, about the welfare of others. She goes to temples, sacrifices and places of pilgrimage. She also visits astrologers, doctors and kinsfolk at their homes. Freely holding festivals, she spends large sums on food and drink. Devoted to mendicants and ascetics, she is turned off by her own people and attracted to those who please her. Able to meditate, she takes interest in ordination and philosophy, though she is indifferent to her own husband and loves enjoying herself at parties. (25–27)

Such are the women of bad character. They are like witches: mercurial, always criticizing those who love them, deluding and ensnaring people at night, plundering them of all they have. Foolish minds engrossed in trivial matters are easily brushed aside. It is only reckless and devious men who can attract such flighty women with love. Talk of luxury and bravery, of various extraordinary gifts, is the best way of winning these women over without any magical devices. For who will not tremble at their wickedness? They are demons of a thousand deceptions in the dark night of this degenerate age. (28–32)

The Tale of Vasumati

Once there was a famous chief of the merchants named Dhanadatta. He surpassed even the god of wealth in his riches. The jewels in his stores were as numerous as those which lie within the ocean. Vasumati was his daughter. With a beautiful body and voluptuous glances that conquered all hearts, she was an embodiment of the love god's glory. (33–34)

The merchant had no son, and Vasumati was his all. He gave her in marriage to Samudradatta, the scion of another merchant family of comparable wealth. The young man enjoyed himself with the doe-eyed girl in his father-in-law's house, but eventually went away with an expedition that had come from some island. (35–36)

After his departure, the amorous young woman would go to the roof of her father's house and disport herself there with her girl friends. Once she saw a man on the road from her mansion. He looked just like Kama, the charmer of hearts. On seeing him, her self-control vanished as if displaced by some bad thought. Her mind awhirl, she was totally unable to restrain her desire. (37–39)

Her girdle trembled. 'Guard your virtue, girl,' its tinkling seemed to say, 'don't destroy your family, like a river its banks.' But who can still a woman's mind once it is in motion? She confided everything in a girl friend, who secretly brought the young man to her. And the wicked girl enjoyed him to her heart's content: with mirth and laughter, growing desire, sexual dalliance and spontaneous love. (40–42)

Meanwhile, the enterprising Samudradatta had completed his business, and returned to his father-in-law's house, eager to see his wife. The day he spent busily with a host of goods, and in festivities with many people. At night he proceeded to the bedroom with his wife. (43–44)

The bedroom was lit with jewelled lamps and scented with perfumes. With an elegant bed, laid out under a canopy in an attractive place, it felt like heaven. Samudradatta was longing for sex. Embracing his beloved wife, whose eyes were already unsteady with wine, he flung himself on her, like an elephant in rut on a blooming lily. But in her heart there was another man. Her thoughts fixed on him and her eyes shut tight, she long seemed to be in a trance like a yogini. While her husband opened her skirt knot, hugging and kissing her all the while, she just sighed and shrank into herself, thinking only of her lover. (45–48)

Samudradatta was a foolish husband. He thought that she was annoyed by his lovemaking and fell at her feet, seeking favours through flattery. For men can be as dumb as beasts. Women may turn away because they love someone else or do not want sex. But men still try to please them. For:

It may come up by itself
or be for someone else,

        but what will lust not do?
        The sun still loves the maiden dusk
        though she will tint with scarlet
        a host of hundred clouds? (49–51)

Vasumati then avoided her husband like poison. Virtually
in a faint, she sent her lover a signal to meet her in a
secret grove in the garden. And when Samudradatta had
gone to sleep, tired out by his lovemaking, she quietly
got up and dressed herself, ready for the tryst.

        The moon, meanwhile, had risen on
        the eastern horizon, and embraced
        softly the twinkling stars.
        Its beams spread forth their glory
        with night's deceptive laughter,
        making nocturnal lilies bloom
        and lotus flowers close.
        The lily ponds were filled
        with the hum of bees
        as if they rejoiced to see
        the sky delighting in the moon
        after the heat of day.
        And the maiden that is night,
        as if abashed, her cloak of darkness,
        by moonlight being pulled away,
        put around her, as a mantle,
        a swarm of drunken bees. (52–58)

At midnight, when the moon shone brilliantly and all
were asleep, Vasumati went slowly to the garden. She
was fearless, but pierced by the arrows of passion, she
could not control herself. An astonished thief, greedy for

her ornaments, followed her quietly as she entered the arbour. (59–60)

There she saw her lover, dressed in a bright and soft garment and adorned with flowers. But he was in a dreadful state, with night birds hovering around him. For, set on fire by the moonlight, unable to bear separation from his beloved, and having lost all hope of seeing her again after waiting for long, he had hanged himself to death from a creeper on a tree. (61–63)

Overcome by shock, grief and fear at the sight, Vasumati collapsed with a moan, like a vine cut down by a sword. She lay in a swoon for a long time. Gradually reviving, she then lamented for her lover in hushed tones. 'O joy of my eyes,' she wept, 'O my lovely moon! What is this I see! Where are you? Where am I and where my beloved?' (64–66)

Thus lamenting piteously, the young woman freed, with an effort, the body from the noose, and, taking it in her arms, kissed its mouth as if to bring it back to life. In an expression of her love, she glued her mouth to her lover's and thrust into it some chewed betel leaf from her own. Meanwhile, attracted by the fragrance of flowers, musk and other perfume she wore, a vampire had entered the dead man's body, and it promptly bit off her nose. (67–69)

Having suffered the result of her wanton imprudence, her nose bitten off, Vasumati returned to her husband's house screaming loudly. The noise woke him up and everyone else too. 'My nose has been cut off by my husband!' she cried out. Questioned by his angry father-in-law and other kin, Samudradatta was struck dumb, as if by a thunderbolt and said nothing at all. The next morning he was presented, by Vasumati's kinsfolk, in the royal assembly, and an angry king punished him with a fine of much money. (70–73)

Meanwhile, the thief, who had seen the whole drama with his own eyes, was amazed. He narrated to the king all that he had witnessed, and was rewarded with a bracelet. He also turned out to be a fortuitous friend for Samudradatta, getting him discharged after showing the people his wife's bitten off nose in the mouth of the corpse in the garden. Thus it will be seen that a wise man who understands the fickle minds and wicked wiles of shameless women will never be cheated by one. (74–76)

Chapter Four

The Courtesan's Chronicle

Then there are women who are courtesans. Extremely cunning, they swindle people by pretending to be in love. Their deceptions can reduce even the god of wealth to beggary. They are like fast-flowing rivers full of waves that sweep everything away in their wake. And, like rivers reposing in the sea, in the hearts of courtesans repose the sixty-four arts of deception. (1–2)

These arts are the following. Adorning oneself, dancing and singing. Looking askance and comprehending desire. Taking things and cheating friends. Drinking and sporting. Embracing and kissing. Other intimacies. Making love. (3–4)

Ogling at others. Acting shameless, angry or agitated. Displaying jealousy, quarrelling and weeping. Not standing on dignity. Swaying, trembling and breaking out in a sweat. Staying alone. Dressing up. Closing one's eyes and staying motionless. Feigning death. Inciting passion by going away. Looking cross. Countermanding decisions. (5–6)

The arts of quarrelling with one's own mother, visiting respectable homes and attending festivities. Those of division, false generalization and playing games. Of thievery and luxury. The arts of self-promotion or being slack; criticizing others for no reason; feigning a headache or sleep; anointing oneself; and displaying garments indicative of menstruation. (7–8)

Being rough or sharp. Pushing out a person and bolting the door. Reconnecting with a rejected lover. Visiting, seeing and praising people. Making excursions to gardens, temples and places of pilgrimage. Planting trees. Preparing medicines and charms for seduction. Dressing hair. Managing the household. Flirtation. Various almsgiving to mendicants and ascetics; and visiting islands. And finally, tired of these sixty-three arts, the courtesan turns to the art of becoming a madam or procuress. (9–11)

There are women who sell themselves for a pittance, even to nondescript customers, and some good-for-nothings seek to cultivate them. The hearts of these women have been burnt out in love. The filthy money they make will be used by some base, naked scoundrel or by some lowly horseman, mahout or villainous artisan. Such a man will become their lover, having cheated on everyone else. (12–14)

Vilasavati and Vikrama Simha

There was a proud king named Vikrama Simha. Defeated by powerful rivals, he was once obliged to proceed with his minister Gunayasha to the land of Vidarbha. There he went to the mansion of the world-famous courtesan, Vilasavati, and enjoyed her, even though she could only be had with a lot of money and his own resources were few. (15–16)

Having observed the monarch's powerful personality, with his long arms and all the attributes befitting a sovereign, the courtesan placed at his disposal a horde of gems and goods for his expenses. The king, for his part, marvelled at her spontaneous affection and wonderful sense of propriety. (17–18)

'It is amazing!' he said tenderly to his minister when they were alone. 'Even though she is a courtesan, she spends so much money on me—as if it is no more than straw. The feelings of such women are tied to wealth, but she has raised them to the level of love. Harlots put on a show of affection out of greed for cash. But if one spends thus, who can doubt her devotion?' (19–20)

The minister felt envious. 'Who can trust in the ways of courtesans?' he said with a laugh. 'Your Majesty, they are devoid of truth, attracted to money and given only to the delights of the moment. With honeyed words they get into the hearts of gullible people. As with the arousal of hope in man, the first contact gives pleasure, the middle part, alienation and distress, and the end result is sorrow. It is the same with courtesans. The infatuation, delusion and confusion they cause is no different from the illusion that is this world itself. Even Hari, Hara and the other gods have not grasped its essence to this day.' (21–24)

After listening to his adviser, and in consultation with him, the king then made a show of his own death to test the courtesan. When the minister had placed the corpse on the funeral pyre and set it alight, Vilasavati appeared suddenly, dressed in all her finery, and leapt into the fire's flames. (25–27)

The happy king embraced her. 'I am alive!' he exclaimed, convinced that her love was firm and true.

Praising her virtues with all affection, he then censured the minister repeatedly. Thereafter, taking control of the immense wealth accumulated by the courtesan, Vikrama Simha built up a formidable force of elephants, horses and warriors. With this army he vanquished all the other kings and recovered his own realm in its fullness, as joyous as the full moon. (28–30)

The king then placed Vilasavati at the head of his harem, where she shone like a goddess, her tresses shimmering in the breeze of handheld fans. One day, when they were alone, she fell at his feet. 'Master,' she said, her hands clasped together, 'you are my wish-fulfilling tree and this slave has long served you. If I have indeed contributed in any way to the restoration of your sovereignty, then my hope could be realized by your grace. For association with the great and pure by nature, who bestow merit on others and remove their blemishes like a place of pilgrimage, can never be fruitless.' (31–34).

'There is a young man who is my lover,' she continued. 'I love him more than wealth or life. He was unfortunately arrested as a thief in the city of Vidarbha. It is to secure his release that I have served you thus, O king. Now do whatever is proper in accordance with your personality, lineage and valour.' (35–36)

The king was astonished at Vilasavati's words. For a long time he stared at the ground beneath him, like someone who realizes that he has been tricked. He also remembered what his minister had said. In any event, he reassured her, and, subduing the king of Vidarbha, had the thief released and united with her. (37–38)

Thus it is that the hearts, tongues and hands of courtesans are many sided, as are their feelings and what they say and do. Full of deceptions, they are essentially devoid of truth. Who indeed can know them? For many are their lovers: one for talking about and one for providing money; one for doing things and one for giving protection; and, finally, one for jokes and pleasure. (39–40)

Chapter Five

The Doings of the Bureaucrat

Delusion deprives people of all they have, beginning with their intelligence. And delusion is deeply entrenched in what bureaucrats say and write. For example, a rich crop of rice ready for harvest disappears moments after it is seen and seized by an official, just like the full moon is by Rahu, the eclipse-demon. Yogis free of delusion can understand the deceptions of this world. But no one can divine official deceptions, even with much effort (1–3)

Officials are the strongholds of innumerable tricks to drain away the people's money. They are like the darkness of the night of dissolution. It is not death but they who wipe out the populace. For they are virtually death's agents, striking people with clubs, or ghouls who go about tabulating accounts and unfurling documents of birch bark. Who can trust them? They are like the buffalo on which rides the god of death. It is a beast with crooked horns, around whose neck even that god's tight noose will not pass.

> Plundered by the bureaucrat,
> the state's afflicted prosperity
> weeps dark tears, which seem to be
> ink drops dripping from his pen.[6] (4–7)

Which man in this world has not been beguiled by
bureaucrats and their artful calculations, as convoluted as
the tresses of the lady Deceit? For people are invariably
destroyed by their own material longings and by
the hordes of illusions with which bureaucrats cheat
the world. (8–9)

Officials are like Chitragupta, the scribe of the god
of death. They work in secret, and have strange minds,
erasing just one line to change a plus into a minus. Coiled
like a snake on the bureaucrat's birch bark, his writing
resembles the noose of death. To their secret tricks only
Kali, the presiding deity of this Iron Age, and Yama the
god of death may be privy. (10–12)

But some of their arts are well known among people.
These include writing in a crooked script, to give it
multiple meanings, and excluding all figures from it.
They also comprise gathering people to their side while
intruding from time to time in extraneous matters. Then
there are the arts of showing increases in expenditure, of
estimating what should be collected as revenue, of giving
and receiving loans from it, and of appropriating the
remainder—not to speak of doing away with the entire
amount realized. (13–14)

There are also the arts of concealing the produce, of
destroying it or showing it as spoilt, of appearing to
subsist on purchases, and of demonstrating losses through
various schemes. Finally, the birch-bark documents may
be burnt and the revenue record destroyed, without
which responsibility cannot be affixed on the man who
stole the money. These are the sixteen tricks of cunning
and noxious officials. They wax and wane like the phases
of the moon, each with a new, but always black-marked,

face. To say no to everything is a tested formula. With
it lying bureaucrats destroy livelihoods in moments, like
gurus of deception. (15–18)

The Story of the Skull

Once there was a gambler. Having lost his money, clothes
and cattle, and abandoned by his kinsmen for fear of theft,
he had been reduced to wandering about. Perhaps it was
his past merits that brought him to Ujjayini. He bathed
there and, passing through a lonely area, saw a temple to
the god Shiva. Entering that deserted shrine, he prayed
sincerely, with sandalwood paste, flowers and fruit, to
the ever beneficent god who is known in Ujjayini as
Mahakala. He prayed for the removal of his insufferable
misfortune. He prayed for a long time, singing hymns
and lighting lamps, telling beads and meditating, without
any sleep that night. (19–22)

Pleased, perhaps by the man's devotion and past
good karma, the god suddenly spoke to him. 'Take, my
son . . .' he began to say, but a skull at the top of his
garland of skulls signalled him to stop. (23–24)

As the gambler's merits were few, and the skull's
signalling repeated and insistent, the god checked himself
halfway and did not say anything. But when they were
bathing and alone, he spoke to the skull. 'That gambler
is a good devotee,' he said, his teeth gleaming like the
bright bridge on the river Ganga. 'How is it that you
signalled me to stop when I was about to give him a
boon?' (25–27)

The skull lived on the nectar dripping from Shiva's lunar crest on account of the heat from the god's terrible third eye. Questioned by the god, it smiled and said gently, 'Listen, my lord. I know that you have a straight and simple nature. But even if you are easy to attain, who ever thinks of god without some reason? This gambler is in great distress. All his activities are stalled because of poverty. He now offers sandalwood paste, flowers and incense as a sacrifice in this temple. A distressed man turns prayerful, one without money becomes respectful, and one who has lost his wealth and position speaks sweetly, bowing to everyone.' (28–31)

'The poor worship gods and brahmins, bow to gurus, and remember friends. Even a piece of hard iron becomes soft when it suffers heat. Similarly, all people turn to virtuous work when their hearts are brimming with problems. But what about those who are maddened by wealth? One who seeks it, O god, hangs on to you by the noose of hope, offering you every worship. And once he has got what he wants, he will never be seen again. For servants intent on their own interests will always become useless after they have secured them. In fact, no one who has accomplished his business ever wants to act as a servant in this world. And once this gambler's purpose is fulfilled, O god, no one else will offer you fruit and water, flowers and other things in this deserted temple. So he should always be kept as a devotee in this holy shrine. By giving him a boon you will be putting an end to your own worship.' (32–37)

The god was amazed as he listened to these artful words. 'Who are you?' he asked the skull. 'Tell me the truth.' The skull thought for a moment and quickly replied with all respect. 'I was born in Magadha,' he said, 'in a family of bureaucrats. But I was opposed to my traditional work. I devoted my life to bathing and fasting, meditation and pilgrimage. I learnt all the scriptures and then gave up my body in the river Ganga to attain your godly status.' (38–40)

'There is no question but you were a bureaucrat,' the god replied, 'you have not given up that remarkable craft and cunning even though you are now no more than a skull.' Then, the beneficent god gave a boon to the gambler, who had just returned from his own bath, brightening the flowers on his vine of hope with a beaming smile. And, even as the gambler watched, the god took that bureaucratic skull off the cord of his excellent garland and cast it aside. (41–43)

Thus it is that a bureaucrat, even when reduced to bare bones, will never give up his innate arts of deception, and will remain intent, like Yama's fangs, on destroying people. Always corrupted by impure feelings, and the chief support of bureaucrats, these arts are as filthy as excrement. This gem-laden earth can be guarded only by wise people who comprehend official cheating, which is a creation of demons. (44–46)

Chapter Six

Accounts of Intoxication

There is an enemy who lurks in every heart. It is *mada* or intoxication. Possessed by it, one neither sees nor listens to reason, but is constantly in a state of stupor. The word is formed of two letters, *'da'* and *'ma'*. In the Golden Age it was *dama*, or self-restraint, in people who could control themselves. In the contrary conditions of this Iron Age of Kali, it has become *mada* in mankind. (1–2)

The chief outward features of intoxication are silence and pursing the lips, looking upwards or staring at others, and dressing and adorning the body. At the root lies the intoxication of wealth. From it are born other trees: the arrogance of prowess and of beauty, of luxury and of high birth. (3–4)

The intoxication of wealth is like the wasting fever. One is stupefied, even in enjoyment, like a person paralysed or transfixed. The person obsessed by his prowess gazes at his arms, the one obsessed by his beauty, at the mirror. Those inebriated by lust stare at women. But the intoxication of wealth makes one blind. It creates a space within oneself where men meditate with their eyes closed, their conscience lost in some inner pleasure. (5–7)

Then there is the strange intoxication of folly. It is without any basis, full of contradictions and devoid of all quality. It makes one mad for unreal things, the madness conquering all else. The intoxication of asceticism makes one look skywards without noticing the impediments on the ground. That of devotion is whimsical by nature, believes in marvels and makes one lose sight of oneself. (8–9)

The dangerous intoxication of learning personifies the agitation of men's minds. It makes one talk on and on, and, red-eyed with anger, unable to tolerate the least criticism from others. The intoxication of power is wicked and demonic. It is manifested in obstinacy, harsh censuring and the readiness to hurt others. Always menacing, it is also ready to confront everyone. (10–11)

Then there is the intoxication of lineage. It is like wisdom that only sees things far away. In relating stories of the prowess of ancestors, one loses sight of one's own failings. As for the obsession with purity, it is always restrictive, forbids all contact and baselessly considers everything to be a pollutant, even the sky. (12–13)

However, all intoxications have their limits. They disappear when their roots are destroyed. But there is one without limit: insidious, addictive and ever expanding. This, the vilest of all and the most disgusting, is the intoxication of drink. It eliminates, within a moment, all the merit one has earned over years. Inebriation with liquor blurs discrimination between what is one's own and what is another's. It regards the learned and the brahmins, cows and elephants, dogs and outcastes, all as the same. (14–16)

The drunkard is unable to distinguish between good and evil. Gold and stone are the same to him. He may have attained the state of a yogi, but, even so, he goes to hell. He weeps and laughs, sings and laments loudly. He is bewildered, and suffers all kinds of afflictions that are mirrored in this world. Does drinking strong wine make him dispassionate? He sees his wife kissing a lover, but is not troubled. He throws off his clothes and succumbs to unbearably disgusting habits. He drinks the moon reflected in his own urine, which he cups in his hands. (17–20)

Chyavana's Sacrifice

In times gone by, there was a sage called Chyavana. He had regained his youth with the help of the twin gods, the Ashvinas, and expressed his gratitude by inviting them to drink the divine liquor Soma at his fire sacrifice. (21)

He was approached by the king of the gods, Shakra, who was enraged. 'Sage!' demanded Shakra, 'don't you know that Soma cannot be offered at a sacrifice to the Ashvinas, who are fit to sit only in the same row as the physicians?' But Chyavana had made up his mind. Even though the king of the gods forbade him repeatedly, he refused to refrain from what he was doing, out of love for the Ashvinas. (22–23)

The angry Shakra then lifted his arm, holding a thunderbolt. But the great sage stopped him with his magic powers, creating a terrible demon to slay the god. Four-fanged and enormous, it looked like death itself. (24)

The thunderbolt-bearing god was frightened on seeing the demon. He sought refuge with the sage, and so did the twin celestial physicians, the Ashvinas, who were urged to do so by Soma, which destroys the mind. The sage was all compassion. He reassured the scared and prostrate Shakra, and sent the terrible demon away, into people's habits of gambling, drinking, hunting and womanizing.[7] He was Mada, and thus does this vicious demon created by an angry sage now live in the hearts of mankind, like a stake affixed there by their dispositions. (25–28)

He is there in the silence of the illustrious and the stares of the newly rich, in the sneers of the wealthy and the raised brows of the voluptuaries. He can be seen on the tongues of the learned and the diplomats; on the teeth, hair and dresses of the beautiful people; in the mouths of doctors and the throats of clever officials and astrologers. He lives on the shoulders of warriors and in the hearts of merchants; on the hands of artisans and the tattooed fingers of students; on the breasts of young women and in the bellies of those who gorge at religious feasts. He is there in the messenger's legs, the elephant's temples, the peacock's crest and the swan's gait. Thus is it that the great demon of intoxication, made even stronger by other evils, forever exists like a crutch on the limbs of all creatures. (29–33)

Chapter Seven

Singers

Wealth is indeed the life-giving force of all that people do in this world. But even it is stolen by slick-throated singers, who are extremely cunning. They are like bumblebees, who, even when they are tired out after picking clean the lotus and tasting the lily, still look to consorting with the elephant in rut. (1–2)

With pots and cloth-covered baskets on their shoulders, with dishevelled hair and many animals in tow, they are like the ghouls who feed off kings. The poor thief can be frightened off by screams in the dark. The thieving singer screams before one's face and takes everything away as he goes on with an entire gamut of musical notes. (3–5)

A group of singers, long silent, will sing with drums in hand, making faces and gestures in strange dresses. The songs are interspersed with hosannas and invocations, with grunts and gurgles at each note, and with self-professed self-praise. (6–7)

One may earn some merit when fish eat the barley grains one drops in the water. But no merit whatsoever accrues from even the millions given to singers. They were created by providence as drains, with great gaping mouths through which the treasuries of the foolish rich can be flushed away. (8–9)

It is not that the cunning singers only display their teeth as they sing. The rogues are also laughing as they extract money from their audiences. Singing in the mornings, they are calm, composed and well-turned-out, with garlands and armbands. By the afternoon they are naked, broke and adrift after gambling losses. But with cunningly crafted songs, containing snares of praise and words as pointed as arrows, these greedy singers will deprive the foolish deer, their listeners, of all they possess. Earning millions within moments with their tuneless and off-beat songs, they then depart, saying sadly 'What has this bastard given us?' For everyone is their prey. This is the curse of Lakshmi, the goddess of wealth, who ignores the virtuous, the twice-born and the aged, serving them all kinds of grief instead. (10–14)

Narada and the King of Heaven

One day, the king of heaven asked the divine sage Narada, who had come to visit him after a long time, about news of the kings on earth. 'I have seen the monarchs ruling in the world of men,' the sage replied. 'They win victories and donate much to charity and religious ceremonies. Their prosperity befits the sovereignty of heaven. Their magnificence rivals yours and that of the gods Varuna and Kubera. They have many times performed more than your one hundred sacrifices, and just laugh at you.' (15–17)

The sage's words filled the king of heaven with chagrin. He angrily dispatched some Pishacha[8] ghouls to earth to rob its kings of their wealth. A group of these creatures then set off, as ordered, to divest all earthly rulers of their riches, with magic spells and charms. (18–19)

There were eight Pishachas. All their names had the suffix *dasa* or slave. The first was Maya, or deception. He was followed by Dambha or humbug, Vajra or thunder, Jhaya or tune, Luntha or plunder, Kharahara or donkey driver, Prasiddha or fame, and Vadava or mare. Arriving in the mortal world, they opened their hideous mouths, and, with great commotion, let loose the system of singing which is both beautiful and exceedingly fearsome. (20–21)

They plundered everything everywhere. This hampered the efforts of kings to hold sacrifices and other ceremonies. For those terrible ghouls concentrated on the ear. Entering that orifice in the guise of song, they steal a king's heart. Therefore only the ruler who does not allow such miscreants to enter his state can hope to preserve his land with its riches and rituals. (22–24)

Actors and dancers, bards and balladeers, conjurors and parasites flit around the rich like moths. One must protect one's wealth from them, for the immense sound of music arising from bands of singers is like the lament of Lakshmi, the goddess of wealth, when placed where she should not be. (25–26)

Chapter Eight

Goldsmiths

Goldsmiths are the yogis in the art of theft. After deep meditation they can demonstrate nothingness, even in a house of great riches. (1)

Gold is the essence of all wealth. It provides ornamentation in prosperity and protection in adversity. But these sinners deplete its value. Their touch dims its glow. It is like the pollution of people by the wicked and always impure scavengers. Goldsmiths use an oily touchstone while buying. Gold rubbed on it leaves but a faint streak. The touchstone they use while selling is rough. This is one trick for making a profit. (2–4)

There are five tricks concerning the weights for the measuring balance. Depending on need, the weight may be slippery, sticky, wax-filled, sandy or hot. There are six tricks concerning the crucible. It may have a double lining, split on being put to boil, absorb the molten gold or be made partly of copper, lead and powdered glass. (5–6)

There are sixteen tricks for deception with the balance on which the gold is weighed. The scales may be twisted or irregular, hollow or weighted with quicksilver, bunched or chipped, knotted or waxed, many-stringed or bent from the front. They may tremble in the breeze,

be light or heavy, dust-filled because of the wind, lifeless
or too responsive. And there are six tricks of blowing on
the fire: gentle, hard, noisy, with gasps, with descending
breath, or with hisses. For the fire itself there are six
tricks: to have it flaming, smoking, crackling, mild,
sparking or primed in advance with copper powder. And
then they ask you questions, tell strange tales, scratch
and feel inside their clothes. They look at the sun and
count the days, laugh a lot, complain of the flies and go
out. They quarrel with their workers, drop a jar, or show
you some marvel. These are the dozen tricks they try to
distract a customer while stealing his gold. (7–12)

To bring out an artificial colour on an ornament, the
goldsmith coats it with a salty paste and heats it in a
fire of cow-dung cakes. He places a magnet under one
scale of an ordinary iron balance, so that it comes down
even if empty while the other scale is loaded. To increase
the weight, he secretly puts gold dust into ornaments to
be filled with lac, but takes it out at leisure after they
have been weighed. He also removes gold dust while
rubbing and polishing ornaments, or he cleverly converts
them into something that looks similar but is quite
different. He does the moulding and filling out of sight,
adds weight, puts a shine on, gives the excuses of loss or
theft for something missing, asks for compensation and
cracks many jokes. All these add up to eleven tricks of
expediency. Yet another is the greatest of all: to slip out
at night, taking all away. Such are the sixty-four tricks
of goldsmiths. They can be grasped after due thought,
but there are others so secret that even a person with a
thousand eyes will not notice them. (13–19)

How They Began

Meru, the mountain of gold, now stands far away from us. Long ago, it abandoned the land of the mortals, obviously because it was frightened of the terrible thievery carried out by goldsmiths. (20)

In times past, rats made millions of great burrows in the golden rocks of Meru, reducing its entire peak to near rubble. Dug up by the sharp claws of a whole army of these rodents, the mountain's base was suddenly loosened. The excavated dust of gold yellowed everything around it. The mountain still shone, but the decrepit state of its golden peak, now pierced through with burrows, made the immortal gods apprehensive that the end of the world was at hand. (21–24)

The sage Agastya observed all this with his divine sight. 'These are the wicked demons slain in an ancient battle with you,' he told the gods. 'They have now been born as rats and begun to bring about the collapse of Meru. They also destroy the hermitages of ascetics, and you should kill them.' (25–26)

On hearing the sage's words, the gods filled that maze of burrows with smoke and burnt out the rats his curse had already damned with incineration. It is these creatures which have now been reborn on earth as goldsmiths. They are practised in extracting crushed gold, night and day, because of their past lives. (27–28)

It is impossible for rulers to eliminate all thieves and bandits. But the goldsmith can always be fully controlled. (29)

Chapter Nine

Various Swindlers

The deceptions of swindlers on this earth are immense.
Fools are caught in them like fish in the nets spread by
fishermen. (1)

Life is the ultimate possession. It is the object of all
effort. So doctors need to be understood, especially by
those who are always in their clutches. They are like the
fierce heat of summer that makes one so thirsty. They suck
people dry, even those who are afflicted with unbearable
ailments. Wishing to increase their own knowledge, each
one keeps experimenting with all kinds of medicines
and kill thousands of patients before he can become
established. (2–4)

The astrologer speaks at length on whatever the
questioner may ask. Making faces to portray his concern
with the planets,

> He calculates, upon the sky,
> the moon's union with a star
> but, alas, is unaware
> who his good wife's lovers are.[9] (5–6)

The clever painter in search of money, having first reduced
all his own to ashes, will then destroy rich connoisseurs.

The metal-worker is naked and dirty, rough and thin. But 'I have acid from the sorrel,' he says, 'and I can extract it from another herb also.' And the cunning old alchemist, with a head like the bottom of a copper pot, cheats bald men with talk of making their hair grow. (7–9)

A trickster, who claims to control the demons Taraka and Shambara, gets a lecherous man, desirous of some woman, to make oblations of wood apples in the fire, blinding him with the smoke. 'Nymphs who fly are easy to get,' he says, 'and so, with some effort, are celestial flowers. Much can be done with mosquito bones, according to experts. With a torch made of the dung of a black horse, one may see Indra's palace in the sky. And, smeared with a frog's fat, a man can become the paramour of heavenly nymphs.' (10–12)

Speaking thus, hordes of swindlers roam around the world, holding out hope to hundreds of men covetous of magic powers, and pushing them into ditches. One claims to be a yogi who can bring a lover into one's control. He offers help to women on every street, but does not even know the basic tenets of sex or the science of love. Other roadside gurus perform tricks for a small fee and thrive on the money and the wives of fools, whom they stalk like hunters. 'Her palm has a line for great wealth, but her husband has a fickle mind,' says one as he rubs the soft hand of a bride from a good family. He looks in a drop of water placed on her thumb for any mistakes the girl may have made, but the thief has no magic, only delusion. (13–17)

Another will put on the show of a trance with a bit of unconsecrated incense, eating and drinking even as he is kicked about. 'The recipes prescribed by Nagarjuna[10] are in the document under my arm,' the glib talker says, 'and they should be offered some incense.' Even so does he take money from others and throw what he has sold them into the fire. They are sons of devils, these dealers in imitation incense. They should be known as thieves who lead their customers only into poverty and loss of position. (18–20)

'That very rich merchant thinks of his daughter like a son, and he is under my influence,' says another swindler to get at the girl's money. More worrisome is one who knows a person's weakness and gets at his heart. He talks in sign language and pretends to be deaf and mute when others interrupt him. Then there are courtesans smeared in holy ash, old Buddhist nuns, and astrologers' wives with their favourite deities. They go about robbing respectable women of their money as well as reputation. (21–23)

'That rich young widow wants a handsome lover like you,' another swindler tells some fool while gobbling up all he has. And there are robbers of time: wily artisans, hired to work for the day, who amuse themselves while the work suffers. There are gamblers who become famous for their skills at sleight of hand, all kinds of calculation and cheating at dice. These crafty fellows then go about their work secretly in other countries. (24–26)

Then there is the relative or domestic help. He earns no more than his food but has large expenses on drinking, gambling and whoring. He should be considered the thief within the house. Also suspect is the uppity outcaste who treats falsehood as the law. 'Who has seen heaven with his own eyes?' he will ask. Then there are the sly robbers of the profit of other people. By promising even higher returns, they will steal the money borrowed from people greedy for greater gain. And there are robbers at law, who are known as advocates; like the all-consuming submarine fire within the ocean, they relieve people, at sea in courts of law, of both money and peace of mind. (27–30)

Some friends are thieves of comfort. They are like bees attracted by the vine of prosperity, drinking nectar from its flowers of opulence, and turning their faces away from the harsh winds of adversity. Others are thieves of the ear. They talk at length about new, unimaginable, but always pleasing things. Then there is the good-for-nothing thief of opportunity. With clever words he builds up the trust of gullible people, creating new situations with praise for their virtues. (31–33)

The most cunning are the thieves of merit. Praising their own, they make every effort to influence foolish people by concealing from them the merits of others. Another rascal is the robber of feeling. He may get himself to be liked, but will destroy love for others with all kinds of tale-telling, just out of jealousy. Others steal reputations. Given to severe austerities and fasts, they run down virtuous people, though themselves devoid of self-control, devotion and tranquillity. Yet others are robbers of the homeland. With beautiful descriptions of the pleasures available in foreign countries, they lead people abroad like cattle. (34–37)

Another person spends the whole day on the sly, with all kinds of strange and agreeable jokes. This is the natural dodger of work. Also worrisome is the parasite who, having eaten up his own wealth and now engaged in doing the same to that of others, spends all his time singing the praises of harlots and whorehouses. One to avoid is the unenviable official. A shark in the waters of rules, he will never accept money because of his great integrity, but takes possession of it in advance. Also the wicked travelling salesmen, who themselves come to your house. All that they offer turns out to be no more than bits of glass once it is in your hands. And those chanters of the Vedas, who sing your praises even if they have fallen into a pit. They seep into one like sweet poison and take all away. (38–42)

The king's servants, who wish to know where they stand, are always deceived by his retainers telling them in private that the ruler looks on them with favour. Other swindlers go from house to house, playing on simple minds. 'I saw the goddess of prosperity in a dream,' they tell them. 'She entered your home with a lotus blossom in her hand. "My devotee will give you all that he gets from me," she kindly told me, for she is very pleased with your month-long fast.' Yet others come to one's house during disturbances or celebrations in the town, or at sacrifices, weddings and other festivities. They enter pretending to be relatives in order to steal whatever they can. (43–46)

If the seemingly considerate servant does not drink wine with his kind, and keeps awake at night, he does so only for some purpose. Some thieves tremble and sigh. Their faces fall and they cannot reply, or they do so in choking words. Others shout arrogantly and ask to be acquitted. They are the suspicious wicked ones, having terrible things to hide. The man to be feared is one who looks just the same, when doing or not doing something, speaking or keeping quiet, in front of or behind another person. (47–50)

Another swindler moves amidst the women of the house like a god of love. He acts simple and innocent, and imitates feminine ways like a eunuch. Also needing to be watched is the person in charge of the treasury, always writing with his eyes downcast, and with dirty teeth and a coat like a vault rat. So too the house servant, who spends all day close by the bedroom, telling tales about the house. He should be got rid of in every case. (51–53)

Money, a source of lifelong concern, will stay undisturbed with one who is always prepared to cover up blameworthy acts that deserve punishment. But a swindler will get to know and amicably obtain every secret from foolish people and make it public for all to see. To destroy the rich, he will leave counterfeit money or forged documents with them, and quietly slip away. As for the poor common folk, who only savour at home whatever money they may have made, he seizes them like a veritable god of death, with weapons, noose and poison. (54–57)

Such a person may also demonize modest and well-born, virtuous and well-behaved people, generally through pregnant women. He fools innocent girls, whose husbands are travelling abroad, with insinuating words and gestures about wicked things, whether seen or not. In a crowd, well-dressed swindlers will simply remove a person's jewellery. If seen, they bravely laugh it off. Otherwise, they make a profit. Another crook will fraudulently take on deposit the accumulated wealth of someone who lives well, and then flee within the year. Others go about dressed in fine cloth and ornaments of purest gold, pretending to be princes dispossessed by

enemies, and being welcomed in every home. A fool
will be overjoyed at acquiring a country bull, when he
has actually been conned by a swindler selling him a
goat. (58–63)

There are people envious of another's wealth and
reluctant to part with their own. A fool will give them
money out of fear, even though he may be broke. A
swindler will go everywhere, cheating thousands of
rich men with baseless documents that he has made to
appear of great significance. Another will appropriate
money from simpletons living abroad for the purpose of
pilgrimage to Kashi and Gaya[11] on behalf of their deceased
relatives. A harlot steals the garments of fools, taking
them off when they are asleep. But she too is cheated by
the swindler who pays her in dud money. (64–67)

Another cheat will lock a deaf and dumb shopkeeper
inside his store and decamp with his valuables. He knows
everything and cheats everybody: one simply in the course
of acquaintance and another brazenly; one by argument
and another by fabricating things. Most successful are the
slippery four-faced charlatans, rich in put-on ostentation
and book learning; in narrating stories and describing
events. Finally, there are the great swindlers who do just
as they please. They come out of their houses waving
their hands and making signals, going everywhere to
enjoy themselves. 'I have just returned from the holy
mountain,' one will tell the elders. 'There I ate the fruit
of myrobalan which gives a hundred years of life. Now
I am waiting for a portent.' (68–72)

These are their sixty-four tricks, a portion of which I
have recorded here. But swindlers have them in hundreds
of thousands. Who can know them all? (73)

Chapter Ten

All the Arts: A Survey

The deceitful arts of cheats need to be known, but obviously not practised. For the wise who seek wealth there are many virtuous arts. Human endeavour has four goals: dharma or goodness, artha or material gain, kama or pleasure, and moksha or salvation. The first art of dharma is compassion for all creatures. The others are helping others, charity, forgiveness, truth, the absence of envy and greed, and kindness. The arts of artha are constant effort for progress, observing the rules, understanding one's work, giving way, skill, calmness and not trusting women. The arts of kama are dressing well, being agreeable, tenderness, enhancing one's merits and understanding the various ways and minds of women. For moksha one needs discrimination, tranquillity, the elimination of cravings, contentment, detachment, introversion and enlightenment. Some or all of the arts in this fourfold division can be acquired gradually. They constitute knowledge of this world, equally for the wise and the cheats. (1–6)

There are five arts that guarantee happiness: giving up jealousy, speaking sweetly, being steadfast, forsaking anger and detachment from others. Seven form the foundation of character: virtuous company, the conquest of lust, purity and cleanliness, service to elders, righteous conduct, listening to good things, and love for one's reputation. (7–8)

Seventeen are the arts for exerting influence: prowess, personality, intelligence, effort, policy, the understanding of signals, boldness, timely help, gratitude, keeping advice confidential, the readiness to relinquish something, devotion, compliance, making friends, gentleness, firmness and the protection of those dependent on one. And three for leading a respectable life: not talking much, not appearing eager and not asking for anything. These are the sixty-four arts that the wise should try to cultivate. Another ten are always salutary: retreat from powerful opposition, submission to it, or confrontation if one has the strength; virtuous behaviour towards those who are suffering; steadfastness in sorrow, modesty in happiness, sharing in affluence; love for the good, mindfulness in case of suspicious advice, and keeping away from censurable people. (9–13)

What is the source of celebrity in this world? Among the verities, it is the guru's word, and among good works, respect for the gods, the twice-born and cows. Among the sins which annoy everyone, it is greed and anger. Among the qualities, it is wisdom. In wealth and magnificence, it is glory. For the distressed, it is giving service, and for the long-suffering, hope. Among the rich, it is charity, and among the comfortable, friendliness. For losing respect, it is solicitation, and for troubled merchants, it is poverty. (14–16)

Among provisions for the journey of life, it is dharma. For those who would be pure, it is truth. Among ailments, it is addiction; and laziness among the things which ruin a home's prosperity. Among the things respected, it is the absence of cravings, and among those dear to all, the loving word. It is arrogance among the things that cause trouble, and hypocrisy among those that make for ridicule. Among the things that purify, it is the absence of malice; among the rules of fasting, steadiness; among things unpleasant, the telling of tales; and among cruel acts, the ruin of someone's livelihood. (17–19)

It is compassion among merits, gratitude among many qualities, and delusion among deceptions. Among the reasons for going to hell, it is ungratefulness. Among adulterers it is lust, and among the causes for domestic strife, the word of a woman. It is cruelty among scavengers, and fraud among the manifestations of this Age of Kali. Among the lamps that light the way, it is the law. For investiture with high office, it is good advice. Among afflictions it is old age; and being ill among the distresses as bad as death. (20–22)

For those devoted to domesticity, it is the wife. Among those who will help one in the next world, it is the son. Among poisons, it is fat. For those with creeping leprosy, it is a passion for whores. Among those who come armed, it is an enemy; among those who ruin the family, a wicked son. For lovely women it is their youth, and for the well-dressed, their appearance. For kingdoms it is contentment, and for rulers good company. It is worry among things which suck one dry; and among those which burn one up, it is hatred. (23–25)

For confidantes it is friendship, and for ailments, regression. For those who would feast on one, it is the absence of restraint, and among wells gone dry, their deceptive look. It is the sincerity of the purifiers, and the modesty of those with bejewelled crowns. Among bad habits, it is gambling, and among the Pishachas[12] of the desert, the abduction of women. Of those with gem-studded bracelets, it is the willingness to give, and to listen of those with jewelled earrings. Among the whimsical, it is friendship with scoundrels, and among wasted efforts, the service of villains. (26–28)

Of gardens, it is their being open to all; of those who speak well, to also look good; and of worthwhile things, a love for the essential. For destroying good sense, there is nothing like an assembly of fools. Of fruiting trees it is their breed, and of those who lived in the Golden Age, their good fortune. Among the suspect it is the royal family, and among things naturally crooked, a woman's heart. (29–30)

Among those who desire praise it is propriety, and love of quality among the users of sandalwood and other ointments. Among that which may lead to grief, it is the daughter. Among those to be pitied, it is the absence of intellect. For the fortunate it is their wealth, and for the famous, the people's love. For the Pishachas it is liquor, and for elephant catchers, hunting. For the healthy it is calm, and for pilgrims, self-satisfaction. For the impecunious it is greed, and for those who live in cremation grounds, their neglect of proper conduct. (31–33)

For the influential, it is control over their senses, and proper policy for those who guard women. Among the perpetually ill, it is envy, and among those who die in inappropriate places, it is ignominy. For the lucky ones, it is their mother, and for those who receive good advice, their father. For the lawless it is getting killed, and for those armed with sharp swords, being cut down. For those who control their anger it is courtesy; for the distressed, sympathy; for the helpful, respect and for the worldly, fame. (34–36)

Among policies, it is loyalty, and among paths to glory, death in battle. Among benefic things it is modesty, and among means of success, perseverance. For those who have everything, it is the merit of their good works, and for the enlightened, their wisdom. These are the sources of celebrity in this world. (37–38)

Epilogue

One adept in different arts,
who understands their inner meaning,
is held to be the best by people,
like, among all castes, the brahmin.
It has been said a hundred times
that the goddess Lakshmi, who
makes use of what she sees,
will especially look at what is done
by one who knows both good and bad
consequences of these arts.
Thus having spoken, Muladeva,
dismissed his pupils courteously
and withdrew into his palace
to spend the deepening night. (39–41)

May this book, *Kalavilāsā*,
playful, charming, full of smiles,
illuminating all tricks and arts
with wondrous tales and worldly counsel,

be by all good people loved.
This work has risen from the sea
of Kshemendra's fantasy
like the moon, and may it always
delight good people's minds. (42–43)

DEŚOPADEŚA
Advice from the Countryside

Prologue

Victory to the god Heramba!
The ten directions smile, lit up
by the brilliant radiance
of the playful raising of his tusk,
slender as a lotus stem.[1]
And victory to the courtesan,
lightning in the clouds of vice;
to libertines, the thespians
in the artful play of crookery;
and to that river of deception,
the procuress, whose forceful current
sweeps away, like trees, the people. (1–2)

My effort is not directed towards those already tainted by
hypocrisy, deceit and such failings. This is merely some
advice from the countryside, which I have put together
in the guise of humour. It is an endeavour for the benefit
of those who may be so shamed by its banter that they
will refrain from venturing into such evil ways. (3–4)

Chapter One

The Villain

Salutations to the villain. He is like a mortar: full of chaff as well as grain, and always fit for crushing both. Friend and foe are the same to him, as are respect and derision, and he is practised at bypassing rules. Thus is he ordained for salvation,[2] but he is also vile, like a dog: greedy for crumbs, fierce in quarrels and always dirty. His tongue pollutes the worthy as the dog's does the bowl. In tardiness, malevolence and harming good works out of ill will, he is like the planet Saturn. Strangely, he is also that planet's opposite: a thunderbolt that strikes mankind.[3] (5–8)

Though a fool devoid of sacred learning, the villain claims to be a scholar because of his past good deeds. In extolling his own merits he is like Shesha, the thousand-headed serpent, and in running down others, like Brihaspati, the guru of the gods. His throat is so afflicted with jealousy that his tongue cannot utter words of praise for the good, even if it is pulled out with a pair of tongs; though in slandering them, he has eyes and mouths on every side. His ears, too, are everywhere, and he hears all as he bides his time. (9–11)

The villain is like the world: illusory by nature; afflicted by passion, hatred and craziness; deluding even great minds. Whom has he not corrupted? Like a person's pubic parts, he is, in fact, a source of shame, addiction and infatuation, and an instigator of desire. (12–13)

Ignoring his own and another's food, the wretch always sits close to his patron, whispering slander into his ear as if it were the cosmic science. Indeed, he talks of everyone's faults. But who talks of his? For who will ever discuss the blemishes in a dirty garment? As if in sport, the trickster even creates pictures in the sky. But he is still considered base, for among the tall he remains puny. (14–16)

> With a villain, influential,
> mad for money, base and cruel,
> holding high office, O people,
> alas, where will you go?[4] (17)

Yet, a villainous fool is preferable to a clever villain, just as a toothless snake is to a deadly serpent, black and winged. Pollution follows the villain as it did the ogre Khara. Both are spoilers of human habitation; arrogant and hostile to the learned; devourers of mankind. Should a villain turn, by some stroke of luck, into a sincere and good person, it would be like an ape in the forest turning to prayer with its arms upraised. (18–20)

To say that a villain will praise merit is questionable, that he will love, unreasonable, and that he will give something, quite meaningless. But to say that he will kill cannot be an untruth. Influencing the master by whispering slanders in his ears night and day, I believe he spreads his control everywhere. What is the worth of anything, in the course of getting which the dust from his chamber door will adorn one's head? It can only be a defect, never a merit. Arrogant with a bit of money, given to grand talk, the villain is a strange invention of the Creator. With eyebrows raised, he maligns, in public gatherings, the reputations of good men, which are as radiant as the expanse of Mount Kailasa. (21–24)

Chapter Two

The Miser

Salutations to the greedy miser. Like the wood of the catechu tree, he is hard, belies all hope of fruit and, in the end, is enjoyed by libertines and parasites. As with the peaceful ascetic, his passions are restrained. He sleeps in the dust, has no attachments and eats but a morsel; yet his greed keeps increasing. (1–2)

Always needing painful effort to please, the miser is disagreeable to all. His kinsmen go to him with faces averted, as if to a cemetery. People spit on the ground on seeing him, for it is as inauspicious as the sight of an owl that does not sleep even at night. As with an angry, swollen pimple, to squeeze a miser hard is in everyone's interest. For, in cutting down on food and clothing, he is an Indra, with a thousand eyes sifting through chaff and husk for food grains and a thunderbolt in hand to chop household expenses.[5] But the wealth accumulated since birth by this old man, his land, house and women, will, in the end, only benefit someone else. (3–7)

Can there be any sweetness in the words of such a dried-up person? Can a home devoid of flavour leave any taste in the mouth? The miser's food is unsalted, and his garment is a skin. His body is rough, for he never bathes. His hair is always matted and his throat dark, like Shiva's, but with dirt. Even if he faces difficulties or obstructions in his work, he will not let go of his hoarded wealth. In accumulating it, he is single-minded. Like a sea without tides and a tree without shade, the ways of a miser greedy for land are out of this world. (8–11)

No donor on earth can compare with the miser. He never eats without bestowing blows on his supplicants and barricading his house. He eats only at night, and then just greens, roots and a broth of plain barley. Alas, he lives in a veritable hell.

> The turban, his grandfather bought,
> the cloak, inherited from a forebear;
> an epoch, even, can't wear out
> the miser's heavenly garb.

He cancels festivals and ignores holy days. His wife never sees salt; for that the neighbours must invite her. (12–15)

The miser dies many deaths in giving even a handful of grain for use in his own home, but feels no pain in taking the same from others. On the feast day of his father's anniversary, and on days of country festivals, he claims to have a fever, or observes a ritual abstinence on account of someone's demise. Seeing some kinsmen come to his house on their own, he pretends to be on a fast as he has quarrelled with his wife. Nor does he greet or respond to a visitor in the evening, for he worries about having to offer him a meal thereafter. (16–19)

Music turns him off. He does not like touching things, hates eating, turns away from fragrance and has no wish for beauty. The miser has thus abandoned all the senses:

In truth, a corpse is better than
a miser quarrelling with the needy:
it stays silent, does not breathe,
and lets animals feed upon it.

Not even a copper comes out of his horde while he is alive; but all of it will depart at one stroke once he is dead. (20–22)

The miser's wife is afraid of spending money. She is scrutinized even while paying the priest at a ritual for their son. But she spends enough on feasts for her paramour. As for the miser, for the sake of some trifling gain he will kiss both the feet of even a scavenger. But then he will cite the rules of purification, and forsake food and drink like poison. (23–25)

Hard-heartedness and indifference, falsity and cruelty, insincerity and ingratitude, all these are the characteristics of a miser. Consider a person to be one when, to save on his expenditure, he runs down even a benefactor, and is censured by good people as an ingrate. Know that to be his house where the oven stays cold, there are no smiles or comforts, no visitors, festivals or recitation of stories. He is jaundiced and constipated; has bleary eyes and a drooling, foul-smelling mouth. It is in his dirt-filled teeth and smoke-blanched blanket that the goddess of wealth resides, for thus indeed does she stay with base people. (26–30)

The miser eats but dry scraps. His teeth are the colour of urine in a fever, his mouth is like an overripe fruit and his body just withered skin. The man of restraint stays awake when it is night for all the world. For the greedy mind it is the other way round. The miser is a great guide in the protection of one's money. The fool bottles it up out of greed for profit. He wears out his sensual urges with the restraint of an ascetic. On considerations of expenditure he interrupts even sex with his wife. But when he does not sell rice that he has already hoarded for sixty years, he forgets the truth that time destroys everything. He danced when there was a drought, and before that when it rained too much, and now awaits a famine or a flood when the price of grain will be high. But the monies he has long kept buried is a wicked act that I believe will also get him cooked in hell. (31–36)

Chapter Three

The Courtesan

> All praise to the courtesan,
> she is like the poet's muse:
> fine ornamentation,
> bold and wanton,
> looking only for
> some money to store. (1)

The courtesan, like a yogini, is without everyday qualities. Free of yearnings and passion, devoid of desire, she meditates on herself and does as she pleases. She is also like a villain's prosperity: fleeting and addictive, averse to virtuous conduct and enjoyed only by base people. But she cannot know the condition of minds stupefied by arrogance. Out of greed she goes with everyone, though it is fruitless in the end. (2–4)

A craving is always difficult to fulfill. With a courtesan it is the same. Who can satiate her? Yearning for everything, she can never be contented, even in old age. And as old age does, she causes loss of blood during sex, makes the limbs contract and plunders people of beauty. Unattainable through intelligence or devotion, through power or

115

contrivance, she can ruin a reputation completely, just as service to a villain does. Like death is her unchaste mind: no gratification for the old, no competition with the young and no affection, not even for children. (5–8)

The courtesan's love is always make-believe, even if she stays with one for a hundred years. She holds her breath like a parrot, and flees when left by herself. Winning one's all with a wager as her eyes dance and flirt, she can delude even scoundrels with the tricky ways of a gambler. Her heart has no good feelings: like a marionette dancing on a string, it displays the artificiality of everything. (9–11)

She is thronged like an assembly hall, with hundreds of interested parties. One comes out, another goes in, while yet another waits at the door.

> Her words are a stream of honey;
> her mind is a razor's edge.
> The courtesan is a sharp axe blade
> that extirpates the customer.
> In artlessness a little girl,
> in sex, mature, in deep deception
> like a crone, the harlot wears
> the face she pleases. Blood and flesh
> cannot ever satisfy her.

Like providence, she transforms people: the intelligent man is made a fool, the rich one a pauper, the honest fellow a thief and a person of dignity one who is contemptible. (12–15)

Entrusted by a greedy mother to a bawd, and tutored with diligence, a courtesan knows the ways of men even before she attains puberty. 'Alas, I have been cheated!'

a lover cries in the morning, having the previous night obtained a girl wishing to be a woman, but still too young. But the wench, though unfit for making love, collects her fee like someone fully mature. She wears false breasts and swindles clients with mere kisses. 'I am a girl just out of the first period,' she tells lovers in the morning, 'and I am sleeping with you today!' Thus does she always earn a feast. (16–19)

An unthinking and unwanted engagement with sex has never ceased since her childhood. Whom can she love? When the plant of youth blossoms in the garden of a courtesan's loins, flowers of gold are gathered day and night. And with young fruit ripening in it because of her merits, she wishes she was another Indra with a thousand vaginas.[6] The marks of bites and scratches on her breasts and the bruises on her lip are witness neither to passion nor to resistance due to modesty: they are left there simply to increase her price. (20–23)

All worldly emotions turn tasteless in the end. Sexual union for a courtesan has no taste from the very beginning, nor in the middle, or at its conclusion. Who can claim her as his own? Her waist has been massaged by hundreds of libertines, her breasts fondled by thousands, and her mouth sucked dry and abandoned by travellers. Having rejected pure food, she secretly consumes the foul. It is clear that the courtesan who cheats the whole world is herself cheated too. (24–26)

She spends the first watch of the night talking and drinking with a fool, and the next in flirtation and intimate gossip. For the remainder she pretends to sleep. Having enjoyed a birthday feast of which her servant maid had told her in the morning, at night she claims to have a headache or that a relation has suddenly died. Thus, if people cohabit with an always unfeeling courtesan in her period, it serves no purpose either of pleasure or of virtue: it just wastes their wealth.[7]

Yet the harlot's mind, I do believe,
attains release in copulation.
For passion clings to it no more
than water to a lotus leaf. (27–30)

As youth declines, the courtesan, now fully engaged in dyeing her white hair, seeks charms for bewitching customers. Whose tutelage will she not accept for this? With the juices from a fish broth, with ghee, milk and garlic, she tries to lure youth back, like she would a displeased lover. Indeed, she must have quaffed ambrosia with the crows at the beginning of time:[8] this is evident from the way she scrubs her face like a girl, even when she is sixty. Her breasts now sag, perhaps because of the sin of selling goods falsely and robbing brahmins of their wealth. But she conceals their droop with due effort. (31–34)

What makes even an ancient strumpet look like this? We do not know what that poison is, and whether we should not drink it too. For, even though old and losing hair, the courtesan swindles fools with the pretence of youth, her bosom thrust out and her face half-veiled. She is like the night before dawn: old, damp, the finery worn out and the starry eyes dimmed. But she has potential for plunder. Her blood has darkened. Her face has turned pallid. Giving birth has emaciated her. Frightened of ghosts, she begs gurus for protective amulets and wears hundreds, made of lac, around her throat, head and arms. But she still sparks in people the fear of apparitions and asks for sacrifices to be made to them. (35–39)

Or, wearing well-washed clothes and often standing at places of pilgrimage on holy days, she sells sex in the garb of a widow. Like a saintly Mahashveta[9] does she come out of a famous temple after worshipping Shiva and praying for a place in heaven. But her tongue, lips and hands are worn out with cursing and swearing, and she shivers in the cold at night, without warm covering or a man. (40–42)

This wicked woman is always well anointed, her eyes made up with collyrium. The traveller who approaches her will never turn back. She wants money. Given to divine worship and listening to the interpretation of dreams, she regularly goes to the astrologer's house to ask about the position of planets. 'I am going to Varanasi,' she says, 'but there is a problem I cannot bear. Without garlic I will not be able to live.' She is an old woman. Her eyes have dimmed, her voice rasps. She sighs painfully and looks pitiable, no better than a low person begging. Nevertheless, she is equipped with the qualities of wizards. She speaks of bodily humours and her mascara enabling her to see through shadows. Despite the pains of illness, demonic possession makes her strong. Her appearance remains elegant, and delightful is the play of her raised eyebrows. It may be proper or not, but the rich man will stay with her till she says: 'Go, now. Come in the morning.' (43–48)

Chapter Four

The Bawd

All praise to the bawd.[10] Brimming with poison, dark and crooked, she is the great serpent that guards a courtesan's sexual treasure from depletion. Able to rob even the kingdom of heaven and, like the sin of a brahmin's murder, frighten the whole world, she is avoided by wise people. Her person is pervaded by the terrifying skeletal image of that skull gatherer, time. She sucks men's blood and then devours them. Within moments, the intelligent turn ignorant. The rich become penniless; even what remains with them disappears when the bawd's gaze falls upon it. She has the power of the vagina and the fearful sound of a pin piercing the ear. In this she is like the Kaurava army, with its warriors of similar names: Bhagadatta, Shalya and Karna. But there was also one called Kripa, or mercy, and of that she has none.[11] (1–5)

Always adverse in her movements, like the awful shadow of the planet Rahu,[12] the bawd can never tolerate those who are radiant, elegant and valiant like the moon. She does not care for past acquaintance or even remember favours. They always end in aversion, like a villain's friendship. Fanged and cruel, she is indeed another image of the god of death as she pulls lovers in. (6–8)

120

She is a living skeleton who crushes the men she approaches, devouring those who are young. It would be an extraordinarily stroke of fortune if she were to perish. For it was in vain that Rama slew the ogress Tataka and Krishna the demoness Putana.[13] Why was the bawd not slain? Indeed, even the all-destroying Yama, the god of death, is afraid of her. For she is no more perishable than deceit, though now only skin, bones and sinews. Her hair was pulled out in quarrels, both her ears torn and her nose cut off. She looks like a female ghoul.

> But the hearts of bawds, I think,
> the mongrel's tail, the he-goat's horn,
> the camel's neck, like snakes and villains,
> subsist upon their crookedness. (9–13)

A source of earnings in their youth, a balance for selling their wares: it is for the many needs of courtesans that providence created the bawd. A worn-out crone, she looks like the older sister of Jambavan, the aged bear in the epic. Can it be otherwise? *Ramayana* is a word that can also be read as the ways of beautiful women,[14] and she is a witness to thousands of them. (14–15)

When she sees a rich customer making several visits, the shameless woman comes out licking her lips in the hope of a big bargain. She surveys his dress and ornaments when he enters, as a butcher does the horns and hooves of a sheep. But her voice is soft and affectionate, as if she is everyone's mother. 'Son!' she calls out, even to an ancient brahmin. 'No one is more lovable than you!' she says to the one-eyed man and 'You shine the most!' to one who is bald. Thus does she praise even the ugly for the sake of money. The inexperienced she loots repeatedly. The more experienced she swallows at one go. Many are just emptied out by this robber of menfolk. She is never surfeited with customers who provide the bread and butter of a hard-working courtesan: no more than the goddess Mahakali is with buffaloes. And the means by which she hollows out a man are many and invisible. Truly, she will even pull out the tongue of one who is yawning. (16–22)

One night she was stricken by cholera. Screaming and vomiting, she found a new lease of life in the embrace of her relatives. 'I am going to Bhrigu's Peak,' she then announced, and, fixing an auspicious day for this pilgrimage, enjoyed a meal of varied flavours offered by the kinsfolk. But she was sick again with fever, dysentery and a tumour, so they took her to the holy Vijayeshvara,[15] from where she returned in a few days. By then restored to health, she drove away the relatives, saying 'All of you here are thieves! Who took away that gold ring?' (23–29)

A lecher has his eye on the courtesan. But the bawd obstructs his wish for lovemaking with the pretence of talk about a former ruler. She is disinterested in someone with no money, and cannot sleep till she finds a method, concealed or obvious, to throw him out. She instigates the poor and foolish pleasure-seekers into quarrels with each other, like an evil fortune out to destroy them. (30–32)

Who created the bawd? An obstructer of lecherous customers, she is never satisfied, even with all your possessions, and remains acerbic despite hundreds of affections. She looks you in the eye and wants your flesh and blood; with a peal of laughter does she make mouthfuls of all men as she puts the waves of Kali in flow. Her name also means 'a pestle',[16] and that is what she is: crushing men as she wanders in the world. (33–34)

Chapter Five

The Parasitic Libertine

Salutations to the parasitic libertine: mean and crooked like the moon of the dark fortnight, artistic but blemished and meritless. (1)

The activities of a double-tongued parasite and those of a luxury-loving voluptuary can cause distress to everyone. Both take pride in the extent of their pleasures. The parasite is like poison. Either of them can cause trouble. To pun on the words, one is passionate and after another's wife, the other is red, and made of quicksilver. I do not know which is worse. But the parasite can clearly be compared to a monkey. The two are always careless, whimsical and quick to anger. To cause a commotion is in the nature of both. (2-4)

The parasite stays within himself. Introspective, meditative, absorbed inwardly with his senses directed at one point, he can attain, within moments, the state of a yogi. But courtesans spit on his face. Good people avoid him. He goes about, perpetually, like one whose appearance is inauspicious.

Clearly, the poor parasite
directs a theatre of deception:
notebook in his hand, he gives,

with his bracelet, entrance cues
to let the others act their parts.

Later, of course, he may glory in the courtesan's house
like the hero Rama did after cutting off the ears and the
nose of the demoness Shoorpanakha, in this case
the bawd. (5–8)

The parasitic libertine is like a cart: untroubled by
coming and going; the wheels always turning; announcing
himself with a rumble. He also has astrological
characteristics: a heroic Sun and a wicked Moon for
women; a crooked Mars and a villainous Mercury for the
mind; in sin as great as Jupiter, in expenditure, as seminal
as Venus; and slow to move like Saturn. Though cheated
by whores, and even frequently thrown out by them, he
returns to their homes like a beaten dog. (9–11)

Though worn out by fasting in some deserted temple,
the parasite makes himself out to be very grand with
false talk of feasts. He wears a heavy cloak in the heat
of summer, the thinnest cloth in the winter month of
Magha, and pyjamas bearing the saffron print of a
courtesan's hand. Adorned with self-inflicted scratches
of love, his sash smeared with some cosmetic, he
goes about exhibiting his good fortune in having slept
with a courtesan. Then folding his sash into a cup,
he lets the whores fill it with mouthfuls of their betel
juice. (12–15)

During the day, the hair of his beard drawn upwards
in the net around his chin, the parasite gazes at the face
of the chief of his temple. A wad of betel in his teeth, his
lips separated, he speaks with mainly dental syllables,
boastfully and bitterly. He talks to courtesans, shaking

his head. The hair on it is his wealth. Oiled in the front and dry behind, it is curled artificially. His bracelet, long used to signal interdictions, he takes in his hand while he explains everything with his fingers, as if he were their source. For all his riches are his appearance. Though he could not sleep at night, as he spent it tossing and turning on a bed of straw,

> As the parasite's wealth is dignity,
> to keep it up in company
> he will describe his own mother
> as: 'This is my water-carrier.'

And, preserving, with an effort, the red coat of catechu juice on his lips, he will drink rice gruel at the step-well. (16–22)

When he is old and gone bald, the parasite goes crying to the courtesan's house, alarmed that the sound of a million knockings inside his head will make it burst. Ruined by debt, oppressed by rivals, marked by harlots' nail scratches, he then turns into a pandit and goes abroad. There, living for barely a month in some Khasa's[17] cottage, the rogue puts on airs with the roundabout talk of southerners. After going abroad, his remaining hair is tied with a sash full of lice as unbearable as a bad omen. But the old fellow feeds on simpletons with talk of elixirs and making perfumes, of sciences about caves and improbable yogas. Thus does this foremost of parasites pass his time: as an alchemist skilled in potions, a dirty packet of ash and a pair of bellows in his hands. His hair spread out and dreadful, his brow smeared with soot, he wanders in burnt rags like a ghoul. (23–28)

Chapter Six

The Student

Salutations to the student. Like Shiva, he is fierce and devours even poison. To use homonyms, one always has a woman on his left in the sacrificial ceremony, the other, in the almshouse; one bears the lance, the other suffers from colic. (1)

The student from a foreign land looks like the skull and bones of death. People avoid him from afar in a crowd, fearing he may be a live skeleton. Of the warrior-class from Gauda,[18] so concerned is he about purity that he does not eat food cooked by others and grunts even at their touch. In his presence even holy sages are put to shame. An initiate observing vows, he bows and prays for two watches, and, wishing to eat, does so at times that accord with the planets. Wearing a holy mark on his forehead, and with food and massages at the almshouse, he looks born anew, like a snake after shedding its skin. (2–3)

He is from the provinces. Tired of his vows, he asks for meat in his meals, for dice games he can win and for the price schedules of courtesans. In engagement with scholarship he is like an aged parrot. For he barely knows the letter *Aum*, let alone benedictions. But, though illiterate, the Gauda student is unbending in his ego: he

127

makes a start with grammar, logic and Vedic studies of the Prabhakara school.[19] (6–8)

The Gauda goes about avoiding the touch of others, his sash tucked under the armpit, shrinking to one side as if weighed down by his load of humbug. His nails are polished with lac, and his garments are embroidered. A collector of discuses and arrows, he is embarrassed by dirty papers. Servants annoy him. He beats them with a stick and dismisses them all, though he tolerates one with a young wife. Proud of the awful squeaking of his shoes, he walks slowly, gazing at the knife in the red sash around his waist. (9–12)

In the evening, this man from the provinces promenades along the street in front of the courtesan's house. The whore and the bawd, the barber and the cobbler, and the dicer who cheats are the five who can undo the knot on this Gauda lecher's wallet. His glow is like that of an unlit lamp. It is more even than saturnine, though indigent singers pronounce it to be like the radiance of Kama, the god of love. (13–15)

The provincial's lovemaking is always interminable, and he is well known for its roughness. A harlot will not have him, even for three times the fee, as she is afraid. 'O I am dead,' she says the moment he ties his hair in a huge knot on the bed. And even if she takes a fee from him in another name, she has to spend four times as much for the aches and pains she suffers in her midriff. As for him, he enjoys her leftover food and wine though even a river is considered insufficient for his purificatory rites. (16–19)

A scarf wrapped around his head in the winter, the provincial student, with his dark face and white teeth, looks like an ape in the courtesan's house. He tries to get a widow too, or even someone's wife. For this he introduces himself in every home with his father's name and tries to gain the confidence of other people's womenfolk. 'Why do you laugh?' the rogue will say to them innocently, as he entertains them with descriptions of food in the almshouse. (20–22)

When he emerges in the morning, he is an image of the god of wealth. Studs of gold gleam in his ears, and a fat triple ring on his finger. But, defeated in a gambling match, by the day's end he seems like a ghoul: naked, covered with dust and making faces. His sash strapped around his belly, his hair knotted, a stick in his hand, the screaming student then starts destroying the hostelry. For who in the almshouse will stand up to this Gauda fiend? His stomach scarred with many knife wounds, he seems ready to kill. Bellicose and hard to control, he does not care for prestige, affection or even danger. That is how the Gaudas of this world go about. (23–27)

The almshouse is closed on the twelfth day of each moon, and, like others, the Gauda must also keep a fast. But he breaks it with fish and meat he has himself cooked. In his own country he must indeed have been a barber or a cobbler, a fisherman or a butcher: for he does not know the litany of *sandhya* worship. When a worthy scholar has had his meal at the almshouse, the courtesans propitiate the goddess with ghee, milk pudding and sweetmeats. But this student is a saint who does his five penances in the forest of the hostelry; and they are womanizing, gambling, back-stabbing, keeping bad company and always starving. Neither a celibate pupil nor a householder, neither a forest dweller nor a renunciant,[20] his is the fifth stage of life: a stage called, for students, the five beauties. (28–32)

Like the ingestion of poison, the foreign student often spells the death of the very brahmin by whose grace he gained admission. A plague for the almshouse, a ruination for the college and a fever for the courtesans, he cannot be controlled by inducements or by affection. He grabs a horn, but it is for milk and yoghurt; he holds a stick, but to beat the cook with. This college student always has an umbrella too. But despite these emblems, he has not been ordained. (33–35)

The Gauda is a thief and happy to be a ringleader. Caught by the workers, he raises his neck proudly. 'I am a *thakkura*, a gentleman,' he says. But,

The old provincial students,
who died with the almshouse
dinners in their bellies,
are there itself reborn as cocks
that crow like trumpets on the house.

Every morning the quarrelsome provincials stand before the grocer, paying less and asking for more. As fish devour the other fish, so do the students divide, within moments, the belongings of some other who is sick: the parasol and the boxes, the sashes, cloaks and blankets. And in the fortnight for memorial ceremonies, the college student eats at some merchant's house, but only looks upwards, as if mounted on a spear, and never at the ground. (36–40)

For,

> This is not a college of villains,
> nor one of high oppression,
> it is just a terrible cave, full of
> old demons,[21] on a forest hill.

To other people, the students at the almshouse seem to be like vampires from the college cemetery, ghouls from the bathing house or fearsome followers of some Bhairava cult. Can a physician be well if he has a sick Gauda on his hands? It is like embracing an angry ape or tying a great snake around one's neck. (41–43)

'Screw mother!' cries the student, burning with a baseless anger, as he does everything at ceremonial baths, gift-givings, fasts and memorial services. A wicked and villainous college glutton with ugly teeth, he goes every day to the shameless governess of the almshouse; he sports with her daughter, and, driving away his own family's servant girl after enjoying her, makes love to the women of a potter. (44–45)

Chapter Seven

The Old Man's Wife

We praise the radiant, nubile girl,
endowed with youth but still untouched
by hand of man, just like the vine
growing in a mountain chasm.
Beguiled as if by ignorance,
by his old age and by desire,
an ancient man asks for the maiden
as a miser does for wealth.
And at the oldster's nuptials
people smile as they explain:
'This clever guy is getting wed
some heavenly bliss to gain.' (1–3)

He comes to the maiden's wedding like a fever: pale and
distasteful, with stertorous breath and failing eyesight.
'My girl,' says the aged father to his weeping daughter,
'this rich bridegroom is possessed of an untimely
senescence.' But she despairs of her youth. 'How will
the touch of these antique hands on my breasts be?' she
sighs. She is a vine. Getting in marriage the bud that is
her hand, the old man will be like a monkey when he
puts his mouth to the fruit that are her breasts. (4–7)

Having set eyes on the young men who came to the
wedding feast, the bride shuns the old groom's bed like

an executioner's block. At their union, the old fellow bows to his wife, his head bent low. She kicks him in the face and he falls down in a faint. He wants to kiss her with his drooling mouth. 'Damn you,' she cries, 'have you lost your mind? You are like a great-grandfather! Are you not ashamed? Say, for whom have I been brought here by such a wicked spouse?' (8–11)

Thus did the bride lament. In words dripping with drool and uttered through his fallen teeth did the oldster beg her to come to bed. 'Alas!' she grieved when touched by the aged lover, and quitting the couch as if bitten by a snake, she fled to the house of another person. Relatives took her back to the bedroom by force, but the bride would no more touch the old bridegroom than she would a scavenger, and slept wrapped up in a separate mantle. The old man lay sleepless: he wanted to embrace his darling but could only feel angry and jealous. (12–15)

At the festival for the appearance of the bride's blood,[22] following her intercourse with a former beau, people sprinkle vermilion powder on the old man's face in the morning. As he carries out all her orders and offers her flowers, ornaments and clothes, she endures him for a while like some bitter medicine. One moment devoid of energy, the next, touching her private parts, the gaffer gives neither pleasure nor rest. And if, by some chance, he does attain unexpected vigour, it means that his very life will depart with his semen. For he is like a worn-out lute. Touching the plump breasts, thighs and pubes of a young woman, the dry greybeard becomes even drier. (16–20)

He had wished for stimulation through a diet of aphrodisiacs, but three years' nourishment on it was lost in diarrhoea and vomiting. His marriage, alas, is finally just the store of his past good deeds. His wife talks about sex, but only takes the name. Pregnant with another man's seed, she always permits the old man to massage her feet, which for him is a feast. And when a son is born, he is so overjoyed that he falls at her feet in the midst of his relatives and, at his bride's behest, even invites his rival to the festivities. (21–24)

The women dance on this occasion. 'A bud has appeared on this scorched and termite-eaten tree,' they say of the old man. But during the wake, on the sixth day itself, the ancient has a massive and fatal seizure caused by indigestion. 'O beloved of that venerable person,' say the women, 'you are blessed in that you now have a son even as you were widowed.' Thus addressed, she does not shed tears, as that would be inauspicious, though some serious well-wishers do say that it is not good for women to lose their husbands during their youth. (25–28)

An old man stricken by poverty and addicted to whoring, but with a young wife, is never seen or even heard of. But he is condemnable as the abode of every disaster. 'What have you got? Where? How much?' asks his wife about his money, approaching him as if he were a thief when his life has half left him. His sexual ability is gone. All that is left is a yearning to touch. The wife berates him with sharp words at night as the old fiend draws in the serpent, his arm, to guard his treasure, and places his hand upon her privates. (29–31)

Chapter Eight

An Assortment

In verses intermixed with the language of the country, I now describe in a condensed form, an assortment of people here assembled.[23] (1)

The Guru

I bow to the guru. He is full of confusions, as is this world: love and hate, fear and hypocrisy, great delusions and fierce greed. His title means 'profound', but even so he is a cause of levity. Short on merit and given to making noise, he is always known as the guru of his disciples' wives. Ordination is so called, he explains, because it literally means waste of money,[24] and that is what he does. 'Knowledge is one's all,' he says as he sings and hiccups. 'O now it is easy in this Kali Age for men to obtain salvation just in play.' (2–4)

The Official

He has already robbed the gods and the brahmins, the towns, the cities, the villages and the cattle stations of all they had. Even so, the official once more seeks plunder and comes to the guru as an ordinand. He acquired his wealth by striking at people with the tip of his pen. They cry in misery, but he has in mind a sacrificial ceremony for the sake of his promotion. The holy mark on his forehead is made with fraud, and all he does is swallow endless collections mixed with ink. He talks and travels a lot but measures up to very little. (5–7)

The Wife of Good Family

At home she watches the face of her husband, whom her boldness has brought to feeling like a slave. Already ordained, the wife then dresses up and goes to the guru. Averse to the touch of an animal and beyond her husband's control, she always returns after purifying herself in dalliance with the holy man. Then she walks slowly as her back and sides are very stiff. Getting home, she gives her husband a kick because the food has been delayed. (8–10)

The Priest

The priest has also been ordained, but talk with the Kaulas[25] has destroyed his caste inhibitions. He has a

mind to drink and comes to the guru's house with a plate
of fish in hand. With gurgles does he drink the wine of
Bhairava,[26] and, filled up to the throat, then rolls about
like a cracked pot full of water streaming out. Having
spent the whole night drunk and puking wine, his face
licked by dogs, he is restored to purity the next morning
by the greetings of other priests. (11–13)

The Merchant

The merchant comes to the guru's house, not as a
seeker of salvation but as an aspirant for an increase
in his wealth. An expert in concealment, he is a fiend
about interest on capital and causes deposits to deplete.
His hands, dirtied by sweeping dust, are yellow with
the smears of jaggery, honey, ghee and oil. Given to
wheedling customers, he is the market ghoul incarnate.
Stinking terribly and filthy with accumulated wealth,
the merchant was made by the Creator as a drain for the
illustrious lord guru's extractions. (14–16)

The Poet

Some refinement has touched the tip of his tongue. Eager
to compose poetry, he comes to the guru for an incantation
to propitiate Sarasvati, the goddess of speech, who is also
his family deity. The words within his mouth are unripe
and clotted, and, though he has no fever, he spews up
verse most painfully, as if it were his life. Day and night

does the poet tear at his heart with meditation on some meaningless stanza. But, without a foray into poetry, the fool will not do his normal work. (17–19)

The Alchemist

His body is worn out with age, his strength depleted with coughing and troubled breathing. Nothing remains of his life. Even so, the adept in alchemy goes to his guru. 'I will fill my people and others with elixirs diffused from my crucible and abundant in gold,' he says. But he will die poor, and, at the end, when the old expert in quicksilver has dysentery, he will be happy thinking that his body is being purified of its dirt. (20–22)

The Gambler

With some fish, rice gruel and vermilion in his hands, the gambler goes to the guru, seeking an incantation to the white-imaged god Ganapati for victory over other gamblers. He is in pain because he cannot urinate, but to cheat the world he maintains a strange ascetic lifestyle: always on fast, restrained and silent. However, even though he looks like the great god, Ishvara, with his ash-smeared and always naked body, a skull in his hand, he is often reduced to poverty. (23–25)

The Fool

Convinced that the guru distributes everything, he follows him like an animal in the forest of other disciples. But he is mindless and no more than a zealot. (26)

The Guru's Devotee

The guru is a cheat but his disciple is a great thief, even among thieves. Always installed in sacrificial halls, his one concern is eating and drinking. 'All hail, O lord,' he says, 'you gave salvation from defilement as the one purpose to the world. I am immersed in sin, master. Save me with your own hand.' With such words of exaltation does he place his head at the guru's feet. But he is a great scoundrel without any devotion, and his eating and drinking show that he is hypocritical. (27–29)

The Lute Player

One of the guru's disciples comes to the sacrificial ceremony with a bellied lute on his shoulder. The rumbling of his music will drive away even the gods being invoked. It takes him the day to tune his instrument, painfully, before uneasy listeners, and then give them earaches with the scraping of his strings. Again and again he looks at the faces of his audience for their appreciation, because the sound of the notes he plucks gives him the pride of Narada and Tumburu.[27] (30–32)

The Physician

The physician's learning lies in the recitation of half a simple stanza, completed with the sick man's money. He comes to the guru, who devours the other sickness, the disciple's wealth. A quack, a cheat and a heartless rogue, the physician is a gadabout ignorant of Charaka.[28] His chief fault is that he cannot diagnose any in the bodies of others. With grandiose words he alarms people afflicted by unbearable disturbances of the humours, and then falls like a fierce thunderbolt upon their homes and treasuries. (33–35)

The Pensioner

He comes from the village to his family guru, a bag of rice under his arm. It is painful to see this descendent of Chandrapida,[29] with his bleary-eyed face and lice-infested limbs. Like a string of fresh snow stained with turmeric powder is the turban on his head. A big toe sticks out of his tightly stretched whitish stocking. Lawyers and relatives have enjoyed the proceeds of the numerous documents of his many debts, and the pensioner, fearful of some public punishment, visits the palace at the end of each year. (36–38)

The Scholar

He is a scholar among fools; to impress them is the reason
he goes to the guru. His long and slow words, spoken
through the nose, produce only headaches. From a bag
loaded with pens, ink and dirty papers, he reads lines
lacking sentence and context with a gloss half-deleted
and contrary. A scholar in only vulgar words, he is
unacquainted with compounds, forgets genders and is, by
nature, neuter. All he knows is antonyms or the opposite
meanings, which is quarrelling. When asked a question,
he obstructs it with throaty grunts and pretended coughs
coupled with spit and snot. (39–42)

The Scribe

The scribe is like the cobbler who always says, falsely,
that he will give everything in the morning. A devotee,
he goes to the guru after writing down the rules for the
worship of Shiva. Confusing letters, scaring scholars by
dropping lines and always filthy, the wicked scribe is
a personification of the Kali Age with its confusion of
castes,[30] scaring of the gods and opposition to sacrifices.
Removing the letter's head from its body, creating new
gaps, destroying the elements and swallowing letters
with the face smeared black, he is also an image of
death. (43–45)

The Men with Matted Hair

Some men with matted hair also come to the guru's sacrificial ceremony. One is bald and the teeth of another stick out. One has Shiva's eyes, one his appearance, and another meditates like Shiva, but without rituals and incantations. Blessed is the matted and knotted hair of these men. Washed clean with herbs, fumigated with incense and deloused with handfuls of ash, it also serves as a cushion for courtesans. When he comes to a place of worship with his matted hair, penances and meditations, the ascetic from the monastery will gorge himself once again to attain the status of Shiva. (46–47)

The Widow

She is engaged in baths, gifts and meditation, and cannot have meat or wine. With the sacred grass, the sesame seed and a silver ring in her hand, the widow remembers the guru as her saviour. Having abandoned unwisdom, she feeds the priests at her husband's memorial rite, and, for the salvation of the deceased, devotedly places her pelvic region in the guru's hand. Adorned with loins plump and shaved, massive breasts and rolling eyes, the widow carries the flavour of a new love. May she give pleasure to all lechers. (49–51)

Epilogue

The sundry things that I have said
are all meant as raillery
to which good and discriminating people
may give ear for but a moment.
Kshemendra humbly does submit
he is not skilled in mockery
but under that pretext contrived
this Advice from the Countryside. (52)

Postscript

What can one say of allaying the torment of serving others, which is understood only when it ceases, and of the treasure of inner contentment? The wicked wish to see, from a distance, the loquacious face of a villain still remains great. People say all is well; it is just a particle of straw on the milk. But with what can the effect of even this minimal fault on the fragrance of these tales be put right? (1)

In the city is someone blind with arrogance and most envious of the increase in another's merit. In the village there is a deep abyss full of rocks and trees, abode of the last remaining bull.[31] It is strange that there is no friend bright with genius, pleasing and clever in thought, fit to respond to the admirers who boldly speak out. (2)

Notes

Introduction

1   This section is based on A.K. Warder, *Indian Kavya Literature* (Delhi: Motilal Banarsidass, 1974–2004), 2:1101, 2:1114–15, 2:445, 3:1218. The work is hereafter referred to as IKL The first four satires mentioned by name have been translated by C. Deszo and S. Vasudeva, *The Quartet of Causeries* (New York: Clay Sanskrit Library, 2009).

2   See nos. 4, 5, 6, 8 and 9 in List of Kshemendra's Works in this book.

3   Ibid., no. 18.

4   *Brihatkathāmanjarī*, Epilogue, verses 1, 3 and 5.

5   Ibid., verse 7.

6   Ibid., verse 38.

7   *Avadānakalpalatā*, Epilogue, 108.12–13.

8   See no. 4 in List of Kshemendra's Works in this book.

9   Ibid., no. 5.

10 A.N.D. Haksar, trans., *Samaya Mātrikā* [The Courtesan's Keeper] (New Delhi: Rupa & Co, 2008).

11 See nos. 11, 12, 13, 14, 15 and 16 in List of Kshemendra's Works in this book. The authorship of the last-mentioned is disputed.

12 Ibid., nos. 17 and 18.

13 R.S. Pandit, trans., *Rājatarangiṇī* (New Delhi: Sahitya Akademi, 1986), 1.13. Hereafter referred to as RT.

14 IKL, 6:4994–5009.

15 Introduction to S.C. Ray, *Early History and Culture of Kashmir* (Delhi: Munshiram Manoharlal, 1970). Hereafter referred to as Ray.

16 IKL, 6:5087.

17 B.V.V. Raghavacharya and D.G.Padhye, eds., *Ksemendra Laghu Kavya Samgraha* [Minor works of Kshemendra] (Hyderabad: Osmania University, 1961).

18 IKL, 6:4877.

19 Martin Straube, 'Remarks on a new edition and translation of Ksemendra's Narmamala,' *Indo-Iran Journal* (2006):49.

20 IKL, 6:4876, 6:4973.

21 *Narma Mālā*, 1.2.

22 K.M. Panikkar, introduction to Ray.

23 Ray, p. 112.

24 Rai Krishnadas in the foreword to *Kshemendra aur unka Samaj*, by Moti Chandra [Hindi] (Lucknow: UP Hindi Sansthan, 1984). Among the works cited are Bana's *Harshacharita*, Damodara's *Uktivyakti Prakarana*, Someshvara's *Yaśastilakachampu* and Krishna Mishra's *Prabodha Chandarodoya*.

25 IKL, 3:1142.

26 Ibid., 6:4969.

27 *Sūktimuktāvali* of Jalhana. Author unknown, *Śarngadhara-paddhati*, 4041.

28 IKL, 6:4877.

29 Ibid., 6:4912.

30 Fabrizia Baldissera, ed. and trans., *The Narmamālā of Kṣemendra* (Ergon Verlag: Universität Heidelberg, Würzburg, 2005). P. Lapanide, trans., *Kalāvilāsa* PhD diss., University of Pennsylvania, 1973. Ann Arbor, Michigan, University Microfilms 1974, Hideki Sato, trans., *Deśopadeśa* (Calcutta: Writers Workshop, 1994).

31 See note 19 above.

32 Note 24 above.
33 IKL. Pandit, *Rājataraṅgiṇī*. B.M. Chaturvedi, *Kshemendra* (New Delhi: Sahitya Akademi, 1983). Surya Kanta, *Ksemendra Studies* (Pune: Oriental Book Agency, 1954). U. Chakraborty, *Ksmendra* (Delhi: Indian Book Centre, 1991).

Narma Mālā

1 This king was a contemporary of Kshemendra. See the Introduction.
2 An incarnation of the god Vishnu.
3 The original text addresses these lines both to the god Shiva and the bureaucrat by using puns to imply double meanings. See Introduction.
4 A tribal people settled in Kashmir, perhaps from the northwest. See Ray. The word also acquired a pejorative meaning.
5 The reference is to dharma or virtue itself melting to enable the ritual washing of the god Vishnu's feet. The story is told in Kshemendra's *Daśavatāracharitam* (5.214–215) as pointed out in Martin Straube, note 18 to the introduction, who also offers a credible explanation of the verses (vv. 1.27–29) partly used in the present translation.
6 See note 4 above.
7 Identified with the present Vijabror.
8 A fragrant gum resin, bdellium.
9 A worshipper of the god Vishnu.
10 According to Ray, the present names of these sites are Vijabror, Baramula and Matan respectively. See notes 4 and 7 above.
11 Wife of the sage Vaśishtha, often cited as a role model for chastity.

12   The sage, so called because he had horns like a deer, was
     born in a forest and had no human contacts till a king sent
     some girls to entice him to attend a religious ceremony.
     The story is found in the epic *Mahābhārata.*

13   An ogre who mainly ate and slept, he was the mighty
     and loyal younger brother of the epic villain Ravana in
     the *Rāmāyaṇa.*

14   This tantrik school combined the worship of the god Shiva
     and his spouse Shakti, who symbolized the static and the
     dynamic principles of the universe. It had a following in
     Kashmir and Kshemendra satirized some of its practices. Its
     most cited spiritual text at present is *Kulārnava Tantra,* with
     an introduction by Arthur Avalon (Sir John Woodroffe)
     (Madras: Ganesh & Co., 1965). The name is also reflected
     in the still current Kashmiri surname Kaul.

15   The writer puns in these verses on the word guru, which
     also has the meanings of profound, large or weighty.

16   The god Vishnu's incarnation as a boar to rescue the earth
     from a demon who had plunged it into the sea.

17   The image is similar to that in *Kalāvilāsa* (5.7), though the
     language is different.

Kalāvilāsa

1   Another name for Ujjayini, also used in the feminine gender
    by Kalidasa in his *Meghaduta* (1.31). See the commentary
    on it by Mallinātha. It was near the site of present Ujjain
    in modern Madhya Pradesh, and regarded as one of the
    great cities of ancient India.

2   Also mentioned in the Introduction.

3   *Eragrotis cynosuroida;* see Jeanine Auboyer, *Daily Life in
    Ancient India* (London: Phoenix Press, 2002).

4   The god of creation. Here he is attended by seven divine sages.

5   Shukra also means semen.

6   This verse has been reproduced in various anthologies, see the introduction in this book, note 28.

7   See the introduction for one source of this tale. It also figures in different forms in the *Mahābhāratā* (3.122.1–27) and the *Jaiminiya Brāhmana* (3.159–61), vide W.D. O'Flaherty, *Tales of Sex and Violence* (Delhi: Motilal Banarsidass, 1987).

8   See *Narma Mālā*, note 4. The satirist evidently disliked music, according to IKL, 6:4970.

9   This verse also occurs in the fifteenth-century Kashmiri verse anthology *Subhashitāvali*, A.N.D. Haksar, trans., (New Delhi: Penguin Classics, 2007) verse 350; and the fourteenth-century *Śārngadharapaddhati* from Rajasthan, verse 4040.

10   A famous Buddhist sage and author.

11   Both pilgrimage centres well known in India to this day.

12   See *Narma Mālā*, note 4.

Deśopadeśa

1   Heramba is another name for the elephant-headed god Ganesha or Ganapati, often invoked at the beginning of an enterprise.

2   A person seeking ordination into a spiritual discipline may need to go beyond everyday rules. Here, a sarcastic comparison.

3   A pun on the word ashani, or 'not Saturn', which is also a synonym for the thunderbolt. The latter strikes instantly, unlike the tardy and slow-moving effect of the planet Saturn in Indian astrology.

4 Also included in the verse anthology *Subhashitāvali*, see *Kalāvilāsa*, note 9.

5 The god was sometimes portrayed as having a thousand eyes and wielding a thunderbolt.

6 The god was cursed to have a thousand vaginas on his body as a punishment for adultery. This sentence was later reduced to a thousand eyes; see note 5 above.

7 The reference is to the three goals of earthly human endeavour, dharma or virtue, kama or pleasure and artha or material gain.

8 A legend has it that the crow sipped ambrosia when it first appeared, making the species immune to age. The source is obscure.

9 A legendary saint. Also the epithet of a goddess.

10 She is also the procuress mentioned in the Prologue to this satire, verse 2.

11 These are puns on the names of the four warriors of the *Mahābhārata* and meanings of the first three: Bhaga, or vagina, Shalya, or pin, and Karna, or ear.

12 The legendary cause of the lunar eclipse.

13 Legends about the divine heroes Rama and Krishna give these as the names of the female monsters they slew.

14 As a pun.

15 See *Narma Mālā*, note 7.

16 The word kuttani, also meaning a procuress, is here used as a pun.

17 A community that inhabited the southern and southeastern rims of Kashmir. They are also mentioned in *Manusmriti* (10.44). M. Vitzel, cited in A. Rao, ed., *The Valley of Kashmir* (New Delhi: Manohar, 2008).

18 The area is usually identified with the eastern part of the Gangetic plain in north India, covering parts of present Bihar and Bengal.

19 It seems this school emphasized learning by rote memorization.

20 The four traditional stages of life according to Manu and other lawgivers.

21 It would appear that many foreign students may have spent all their lives at almshouses, which were supported by local charities.

22 Presumably hymenal.

23 The brief comments on various characters now mentioned are worth comparison with longer ones in *Narma Mālā* and *Kalāvilāsa*.

24 A play on the word for ordination, diksha, implying that its first syllable stands for dīnāra or coin, and the second for kshaya or waste.

25 See *Narma Mālā,* note 14.

26 A fierce form of the god Shiva.

27 Divine musicians.

28 A celebrated exponent of Indian medicine. This is a pun on his name, a word which could also mean 'vagrant'.

29 The name of a king in an earlier dynasty. The impression conveyed here is of a person of noble lineage who has come down in life. Also mentioned in the introduction to this book. See IKL, 6: 4901.

30 A play on the word varna which means colour or letter, and also caste or class.

31 The verses, here rendered in prose, follow the epilogue in the original text. See the introduction for a comment, which can only be speculative in the absence of more data.

List of Kshemendra's Works

Works Located in Manuscript, Edited and Printed

Abridgements

1 *Ramāyaṇamanjari*. Kavyamala 83. Mumbai: N.S. Press, 1903.

2 *Bhāratamanjari*. Kavyamala 18. Mumbai: N.S. Press, 1903.

3 *Brihatkathāmanjari*. Kavyamala 69. Mumbai: N.S. Press, 1903.

Poetics

4 *Auchitya Vichāra Charchā*. Varanasi: Chowkhamba Vidyabhawan, 1992.

5 *Kavikanthābharaṇa*. Varanasi: Motilal Banarsidass, 1969.

6 *Suvrittatilaka*. Kavyamala 2. Mumbai: N.S. Press, 1886.

Satires

7 *Kalāvilasā*. Kavyamala 1. Mumbai: N.S. Press, 1886.

8 *Samaya Mātrikā*. Kavyamala 10. Mumbai: N.S. Press, 1886.

9 *Narmamālā*. Kashmir Sanskrit Series 40. Srinagar: 1923.

10 *Deśopadeśa*. Kashmir Sanskrit Series 40. Srinagar: 1923.

Didactic Works

11   *Nitikalpataru*. Pune: Bhandarkar Oriental Research Institute, 1956.
12   *Darpadalana* in *Minor Works of Ksemendra*. Hyderabad: Osmania University, 1961.
13   *Chaturvargasaṃgraha* in *Minor Works of Ksemendra*. Hyderabad: Osmania University, 1961.
14   *Chārucharya* in *Minor Works of Ksemendra*. Hyderabad: Osmania University, 1961.
15   *Sevyasevakopadeśa* in *Minor Works of Ksemendra*. Hyderabad: Osmania University, 1961.
16   *Lokaprakāśa*. Kashmir Sanskrit Series 75. Srinagar: 1947.

Others

17 *Avadānakalpalatā*. Biblothica Indica 1.2. Kolkata: 1940.
18 *Daśavataracharita*. Delhi: Munshiram Manoharlal, 1983.

Works Known Only through Citations

1   *Amritataranga*
2   *Avasarasara*
3   *Lāvaṇyavati*
4   *Padyakādambari*
5   *Vinayavalli*
6   *Muktāvali*
7   *Pavana Panchāśika*
8   *Munimata Mimāmsā*
9   *Śhashivamśa*
10   *Lalitaratnamālā*
11   *Kanakajānaki*
12   *Chitrabhārata*
13   *Nitimālā*
14   *Kavikarṇikā*

15   *Vātsyāyana Sūtra Sāra*
16   *Nripāvali*

The last mentioned of these is a history of Kashmir as mentioned in the Introduction. The titles at 6, 8 and 14 could be works on poetics; 1, 2 and 7, descriptive poems; 11 and 12, descriptive plays based on incidents in the two epics; 5 and 13, didactic works on conduct; 10 derived from Harsha's ninth-century play *Ratnāvali*; and 4 and 15 as already mentioned in the introduction. These are conjectures based on scholarly comments needing confirmation with further data.